BEST OF IRISH
TRADITIONAL
COOKING

DELICIOUS MODERN RECIPES

Best of
Irish

BASED ON TRADITIONAL IRISH COOKING

PRAISE FOR THE *BEST OF IRISH* COOKBOOKS:
'This series is fabulous and highly recommended. The
books are packed full of information ... A handy and very
neat addition to any kitchen shelf'
Books Ireland
'Exciting Irish cookbook series.
Easy to follow, zippy and well presented'
Carla Blake, Irish Examiner
'An easy-to-carry-gift to bring home as a souvenir of a visit'
RTÉ Guide
'Sound recipes with an Irish flavour ...
And they are quite straightforward'
Georgina Campbell, Irish Independent

BIDDY WHITE LENNON is a founder member and currently Chairwoman of the Irish Food Writers Guild. Her previous cookbooks include *The Leaving Home Cookbook*, *Irish Traditional Cooking* and *The Eating at Home Cookbook*. She has written and presented a ten-part television series on healthy eating for the Irish Department of Health.

Biddy writes regularly for *Food and Wine Magazine*, has a cookery column in the *Irish Farmers' Journal* and a column in *Woman's Way* magazine. She gives cookery demonstrations all over Ireland and is a freelance contributor to many publications and a regular broadcaster on television and radio on subjects as varied as health, social welfare, fashion, interiors and travel.

As an actress, she is perhaps best known in Ireland for her portrayal of Maggie in the hugely popular RTÉ television series, *The Riordans*, a role she played for fifteen years. She continued to act in the series when it moved to radio and also co-wrote many episodes with her husband, later writing for the TV series *Glenroe*.

Best of
Irish
Traditional
COOKING

BIDDY WHITE LENNON

THE O'BRIEN PRESS

DUBLIN

First published 2002 by The O'Brien Press Ltd,
20 Victoria Road, Dublin 6, Ireland.
Tel: +353 1 4923333; Fax: +353 1 4922777
E-mail: books@obrien.ie
Website: www.obrien.ie
Reprinted 2003.

ISBN: 0-86278-758-0

British Library Cataloguing-in-Publication Data
White Lennon, Biddy
Best of Irish traditional cooking
1.Cookery, Irish
I.Title II.O'Hara, Anne III.Irish traditional cooking
641.5'9'415

2 3 4 5 6 7
03 04 05 06 07 08

Editing, layout, typesetting, design: The O'Brien Press Ltd
Author photograph: Peter Orford
Internal illustrations: Anne O'Hara
Cover photography: Walter Pfeiffer
Printing: Cox & Wyman Ltd

Contents

Introduction

When I wrote my first book about traditional Irish cooking, I divided ten thousand years of Irish social history into six roughly chronological periods, each dominated by one staple Irish foodstuff: fish, shellfish, crustaceans and seaweed; white meats – milk, butter and cheese; grains, vegetables and fruits; meat and game; the potato; alcoholic drinks.

However arbitrary this might have seemed at the time, it made sense to me as I thought long and hard about our attitudes to food and cooking and to our food traditions. More importantly, it seemed to make sense to others; to several professional historians and food writers I respected and to countless other people, including many teachers and food professionals, who were kind enough to write to me.

I wrote then that traditional Irish food was alive and well and growing in status once more. I'm delighted to report that, a decade or so on, my optimism has proved well-founded. It has never been easier, if you do your research in advance, to dine well in Ireland on dishes that still reflect the primacy of those six main staple foods approached in the 'traditional' way. A new generation of extremely talented Irish chefs have grabbed their culinary heritage and developed it – given it 'spin' is the fashionable phrase – into a recognisable new Irish cuisine.

I do applaud this. I regularly eat their 'gourmet Irish stews' with enormous relish and a genuine appreciation of what they have done to what was, and still is, a great, simple, white stew. But my appreciation of their achievement is based on my knowledge of what a real Irish stew tastes like – it's wonderful without any 'spin' at all, if it is properly cooked using the best ingredients! This book attempts to take you back to the simple way of preparing these dishes so that you, too, can appreciate what the best Irish chefs are now doing with them. I have included a few of their recipes as well, to give an idea of what they're at.

Historically, there is no such thing as a definitive recipe for any traditional Irish dish. We do have the 'receipts' of some very individual Irish cooks who were employed in one or other Big House. These usually record the way they prepared some dishes but most often are a simple record of the ingredients used. What is constant, however, are their methods of preparation.

After the heroic age with its freshly dug seething pits, or *fulucht fiadh*, which were filled with water and brought up to seething point with fire-heated stones, the traditional Irish home had very limited means of cooking: an open turf fire, a large iron pot which could be suspended at different heights above the fire or its embers, a flat iron griddle which could be similarly adjusted, and sometimes a chimney, but more usually just the rafters, for smoking. The relatively big house of a prosperous farmer might have a spit for roasting in front of an open fire and some kind of crude, directly-heated oven, usually off the chimney.

Cooking techniques were inevitably simple: designed for the daily routine – griddle breads or 'cakes'; or for extending the life of foodstuffs – smoking, salting and curing; and then dishes either for 'keeping' (how long, after all, does a hard-working day, a point-to-point horse race, a hunt, or an Irish funeral last?); or for quick and simple meals. Most dishes were one-pot, in the style of peasant cooking everywhere, and for which the potato was supremely suited. You can be sure they were based on whatever ingredients happened to be in season, or available. 'You'll just have to take pot luck' is still the disarming apology of an Irish housewife, no matter how good a cook, when called upon to feed unexpected visitors.

The recipes chosen for this little book, even those of famous Irish chefs, are not true restaurant dishes but dishes that are still cooked and eaten in Irish homes: traditional potato dishes, breads and baking that remain popular, and dishes once cooked only in the Big House. These, as we become increasingly prosperous, confident, and proud of our Irish food culture, are regularly enjoyed by everyone and even cooked by those who can spare time out from the demands of the Celtic Tiger.

It would be foolish to deny that contemporary Ireland has multi-cultural tastes when it comes to food. Many of our children are more familiar with pasta, pizza, pâté, Chinese stir-fry and Thai noodles than with corned beef and herrings. But, in a sense that's how it has always been. We've always taken from other food cultures whatever we wanted and given the dishes our very particular Irish 'spin'. We remain a food-exporting nation; our meat, seafoods and dairy produce are exported all over the world and there is no reason why our way of cooking them should not be equally popular.

seafood chowder

Chowder is the only really popular Irish fish soup today and turns up on lunchtime menus throughout the country — possibly because of the cream and potatoes. It's usually eaten with crusty bread, making it something of a meal in itself.

SERVES 6

Ingredients:

1 tablesp butter or olive oil

110 g/4 oz streaky bacon, finely chopped

225 g/8 oz onions, finely chopped

2 bay leaves

450 g/1 lb floury potatoes, peeled and finely chopped

500 ml/16 fl oz/2 cups fish stock

300 ml/10 fl oz/1¼ cups milk

700 g/1½ lb firm-fleshed white fish, skinned, boned, cut into bite-sized pieces

90 g/3 oz/smoked cod or haddock, skinned, boned, cut into bite-sized pieces

150 ml/5 fl oz/ cup cream

700 g/1½ lb mussels, cockles, clams, cooked and shelled

225 g/½ lb prawns, scallops, shrimp, cooked and shelled

lots of fresh parsley and/or chives, finely chopped

Method:

Melt the butter in a large pot and cook the bacon until crisp. Add onions and cook until translucent (not browned). Add potatoes, stock and milk, and simmer until the potatoes are tender. If the potatoes have not disintegrated sufficiently to thicken the liquid to your taste use a fork and mash them a little into the soup. Add the fish and simmer for 2-3 minutes. Add the cream and simmer for 30 seconds. Finally, add the shellfish. As soon as the liquid reaches simmering point remove the pot from the heat. Season to taste with salt, freshly ground pepper and most of the herbs. Serve hot sprinkled with the remaining herbs.

POTATO SOUP

Don't be fooled by the ingredients into thinking this is the same as French vichyssoise. Irish potato soup has far more potatoes, is made on milk not cream, and eaten hot not cold.

SERVES 6

Ingredients:

1 kg/2¼ lb floury potatoes, peeled and quartered (if large)

2 medium onions, peeled and chopped

or

2 large leeks, cleaned and sliced finely

1 stick celery, finely chopped (optional)

2 tablesp butter

1.5 ltrs/2⅓ pts/6 cups (approx) half milk/half water, or poultry stock

Garnish:

3–4 tablesp chopped parsley or chives

a little lightly-whipped cream (optional)

Method:

Melt the butter in a heavy pan over a gentle heat and sweat the onions or leeks (and the celery) until soft but not brown. Add the liquid and potatoes to the pan, season with salt and freshly ground black pepper and simmer until the potatoes are tender. Purée in a foodmill or food processor, return to the pan and reheat. Check seasoning and serve hot sprinkled with herbs and a little cream lightly stirred through.

Variations:

This basic recipe can be enhanced by garnishing with chopped, crisply-cooked bacon, or with a little leftover cooked ham, or even with diced, cooked sausage.

It can also be given a seafood treatment with chopped cooked prawns, scallops, mussels or clams.

Ring the changes with different fresh herbs like dill, mint, marjoram, or even a little rosemary.

wheelbarrow soup

Molly Malone was a famous fish-seller in Dublin's fair city who, according to the song 'wheeled her wheelbarrow through streets broad and narrow, crying cockles and mussels alive, alive-o'. The song is an unofficial Dublin anthem – and a rallying call of the Irish international rugby football team.

When a bronze statue representing Molly was unveiled at the Trinity College end of Grafton Street, many citizens considered her rather 'better-endowed' than the girl of their romantic imaginings. Dublin wags (who must immediately name every piece of street furniture and statuary in the city) promptly christened her 'the tart with the cart'!

SERVES 6–8

Ingredients

about 2 dozen cockles

about 3 dozen mussels

3 tablesp butter

3 tablesp white flour

3 tablesp onion, peeled and very finely chopped

2 cloves garlic, peeled, crushed and finely chopped (optional)

cooking liquid from the cockles and mussels

sufficient milk to make this up to 1.5 ltrs/2 pts/6 cups liquid

Garnish:

2 tablesp chopped chives

2 tablesp chopped parsley

a little lightly-whipped cream (optional)

Method:

Scrub and clean the shellfish thoroughly to get rid of any grit, sand or adhering small barnacles. Discard any that are open or do not close when tapped lightly. Place in a large, wide pot. Barely cover with salted water. Bring to the boil and when the shells have opened remove from the heat. Discard any that have not opened. It's simple to slip the flesh from the shells but do it over a bowl because you want to save any juices from the shells. Add this juice to the liquid in the pot, then use a fine strainer to strain all the cooking liquid into a bowl (this step is necessary to remove any remaining sand or grit). Melt the butter in a heavy-bottomed pan and soften the onion and garlic over a gentle heat. Stir in the flour and add the shellfish liquid and the milk. Stir (or whisk) until blended and free of lumps. Simmer for about 5 minutes to cook the flour. Add the shellfish and just heat them through.

Serve at once garnished with the herbs and a little cream.

Cook's Tip:

It's sad but true that nowadays clams are easier to buy in Dublin than cockles; fortunately they make a perfectly good substitute.

SPRING TONIC NETTLE SOUP

Nettles are a traditional spring tonic — an ancient Irish way of flushing toxins from the system that actually has some scientific basis. Nettles are rich in iron and also valuable in the treatment of arthritis. Pick only the tender tops (never use tops which have flowered) and use gloves when picking them. It is possible, by harvesting frequently, to keep young nettle tops going right through until the early summer.

SERVES 6

Ingredients:

350 g/12 oz/2 cups floury potatoes, peeled and cubed

150 g/5 oz/1 cup mild onion, peeled and finely chopped

3 cups (closely packed) nettle tops, washed and roughly chopped

2 tablesp/¼ stick butter (**or** bacon, duck, or goose fat)

1.5 ltrs/2⅓ pts/6 cups chicken **or** turkey stock

Garnish:

2 tablesp chopped fresh parsley or chives

a little cream, lightly whipped

Method:

Melt the butter in a large pot and sweat the onion and potato for about 10 minutes over a gentle heat. Wash the nettle tops, drain them and add them to the pot to simmer for 5 minutes only (any longer and the bright green colour fades and a rather strong taste develops). Test for tenderness — don't worry, they don't sting after cooking! Purée the soup until smooth in a foodmill or food processor. Return to the pan and reheat.

Serve garnished with a swirl of cream and the chopped herb of your choice.

Variation:

Before cultivated cabbage was introduced, watercress was the traditional accompaniment to boiled bacon and it still grows wild all over Ireland. It can be used in place of nettles but nowadays you should only buy watercress that has been commercially farmed. Use double the amount of watercress to replace the nettles.

CLONAKILTY BLACK PUDDING

WITH CARAMELISED APPLES AND BALSAMIC VINEGAR

Black pudding is an ancient, much loved, and still widely-eaten food. There are regional variations in style and flavourings, and family butchers throughout the country still have their own recipes. Edward Twomey of Clonakilty in County Cork uses a local recipe to produce and market his wonderful pudding, which is mealy (pinhead oatmeal) and onion-flavoured. He brought it to the attention of leading Irish chefs, who now do all kinds of tasty things with it. A few years ago Edward was given a lifetime achievement award by the Irish Food Writers Guild and this recipe was developed specially by The Commons Restaurant in Dublin to be served at the awards luncheon.

SERVES 4

Ingredients:

480 g/1 lb Clonakilty black pudding

3 Granny Smith apples, peeled

100 g/3½ oz Irish honey

200 ml/7 fl oz/¾ cup balsamic vinegar

olive oil (to taste)

mixed salad leaves, washed and dried

Method:

Core the apples and cut each one into 6 wedges. Using a non-stick, ovenproof pan, cook the wedges gently in the honey until caramelised. Add the vinegar and transfer the apple wedges to the oven to cook at 170°C/350°F/Gas 4 for 5 minutes. Use a palette knife to remove them from the pan and place on serving plates. Make the salad dressing by mixing the cooking juices with olive oil (to taste) and season with salt and pepper. Use a sharp knife to slice the puddings (about 2 cm/1 inch slices) and peel off the casing carefully. Place the pieces on a flat baking sheet and cook in a hot oven for about 5 minutes or until warm through. Arrange on serving plates with the apple wedges and dressed salad leaves. Serve warm.

GRILLED BLACK PUDDING

WITH HERBED POTATO PANCAKES AND MUSTARD

This recipe comes from Chris Daly, head chef of Tinakilly House, *Rathnew,* County Wicklow.

SERVES 4

Ingredients:

12 slices of Clonakilty black pudding, 1 cm/½ inch thick

For the Potato Pancakes:

150 g/5 oz floury potatoes, cooked and mashed while hot

90 g/3 oz/¾ cup plain white flour

1 large egg

2 tablesp fresh herbs, chopped

3-4 tablesp milk

a little grated nutmeg

15 g/½ oz/1 level tablesp butter

a little oil

Garnish:

fresh parsley, wholegrain mustard

Method:

Grill the black pudding until just beginning to crisp and keep warm.

In a food processor mix the potatoes, flour, egg, herbs, and enough milk to loosen the consistency and make a thick batter. Season with salt, black pepper and freshly grated nutmeg. Heat a heavy pan and when hot add the butter and a little oil. Using a dessertspoon, measure out 12 small pancakes. Cook on each side until golden brown and cooked through.

Place 3 pancakes on each plate with the black pudding on top. Garnish with fresh parsley and wholegrain Irish mustard – a whiskey-flavoured one is especially good with this dish. You may, if you wish, loosen the mustard with a little cream.

GRILLED GOATS CHEESE

Most Irish farmhouse goats cheeses are seasonal – made from spring through autumn. Well-known names are Mine Gabhar, St Tola, Boilie, Poulcoin, Corleggy, Oisin, Old MacDonald's. Some are sold to be eaten very fresh, others can be eaten at any stage of ripeness you like. Cheeses made from the milk of goats and sheep are the most suitable for grilled or baked dishes as they do not curdle or become tough as easily as cheese made from cows' milk.

With so many fine cheeses now available it is no surprise that a warm goats cheese salad has become a much-liked Irish starter on many restaurant menus. There's no definitive recipe, each chef or home cook puts their own spin on the dish, particularly when it comes to accompaniments and dressings.

SERVES 4

Ingredients:

225 g/8 oz/1 cup fresh Irish goats cheese

fresh, soft salad leaves of choice

2-3 tablesp fresh herbs (flat-leafed parsley, marjoram, Bowles' mint and chives)

½ red pepper, roasted, deseeded, skinned and cubed

4 small rounds of dense-textured bread, lightly toasted

1 small clove of garlic, peeled (optional)

4 teasp hazelnut oil

2 tablesp vinaigrette dressing

Method:

Toast the bread lightly and rub with a cut clove of garlic.

Divide the cheese into 4 servings of about 60 g/2 oz/¼ cup each. Place on the toasted bread with a few pieces of the red pepper on top and drizzle with hazelnut oil.

Clean, dry, and tear the salad leaves and herbs into bite-sized pieces. Dress with the vinaigrette just before serving and use these leaves to dress the plates. Heat the cheese under a very hot grill for 1 minute. Serve at once.

Variation:

The cheese can be set on a round of baked puff pastry, or placed in a ready-baked filo (phyllo) pastry nest. The dish can be garnished with a little pesto, or a spoonful of onion marmalade.

cashel blue cheese dressing for salad

Cashel Blue is one of Ireland's famous farmhouse cheeses. It is made in Fethard, County Tipperary, near the famous Rock of Cashel. This dressing is particularly good for a green salad to be served with cold baked ham.

Ingredients:

2 cloves garlic, peeled, crushed and chopped

3-4 tablesp olive oil

1 tablesp wine vinegar

30 g/1 oz/2 level tablesp Cashel Blue cheese

Method:

Heat a little of the olive oil in a small pan, add the garlic and cook gently for one minute. Tip into a bowl and add the cheese, then beat until you have a paste. Gradually add the rest of the oil and vinegar and whisk until smooth.

smoked salmon

In the sagas, the tale is told of a salmon swimming beneath a hazel tree, the Tree of Knowledge; some nuts fell and landed on the salmon's back, giving the salmon its spots as well as transferring knowledge from the hazel tree to the fish – known ever after as the fish of knowledge. Aeons later, Fionn MacCumhaill, while a trainee warrior, caught a salmon and started to cook it for his master. Seeing a blister rise upon the skin, he burst it with his thumb and burned his skin. As he sucked his thumb to ease the pain, the fish's knowledge transferred to him. He was promptly elected leader of the Fianna and a great feast was held to celebrate his election. Thousands of years later, the salmon is still the Irish fish of feasting and celebration.

Wild Irish salmon – in season from January to August – is eaten fresh, smoked or pickled. It is highly prized when smoked, is very expensive, and worth every penny. Farmed salmon, available all year round, is one of our most popular fishes and its relatively low cost means that smoked salmon (even if farmed) is no longer a rare treat but an everyday 'fast food'. Fresh farmed salmon is now regularly cooked in the home.

SERVES 4

Ingredients:

450 g/1 lb smoked salmon

1 large lemon

freshly ground black pepper

brown soda bread and butter

a few mixed green salad leaves to garnish

Method:

Slice the salmon very thinly and lay on plates. Dress the salad leaves lightly with vinaigrette. Serve with buttered slices of brown soda bread, lemon wedges and a pepper mill; allow everyone to grind black pepper over the salmon to their taste.

smoked salmon
with potato cakes

This can be served as a starter or a light snack, or for breakfast.

SERVES 4

Ingredients:

8 slices of smoked salmon

8 small potato cakes, cooked

125 ml/4 fl oz/½ cup sour cream

1 tablesp chives, finely chopped

For the Potato Cakes:

450 g/1 lb floury potatoes, cooked, and mashed hot

60-175 g/2-6 oz/½-1½ cups plain white flour

½ teasp salt

2 tablesp butter, melted

60 ml/2 fl oz/¼ cup milk (approximately)

Method:

Heat the cooked potato cakes (*see* below) in the oven or on a pan set over a low heat. Mix the sour cream and chives and season with black pepper. On each potato cake place a slice of salmon, folded over so that it fits neatly on top. Top with little sour cream.
Serve while the potato cakes are still warm.

potato cakes

Method:

Keep back a couple of tablespoons of the flour. Mix all the other ingredients together, adding just enough milk to make a fairly firm dough. Sprinkle the flour on a flat surface and roll the dough out until it is 0.5-1 cm /¼-½ inch thick. Cut into square, triangular or round shapes, as you wish. Bake on an ungreased griddle (or heavy frying pan) until lightly brown on both sides. Serve hot from the pan, or reheat by frying in a little bacon fat or butter, or grill spread with very little butter until warmed through.

Makes 8-12 depending on the thickness and shape chosen.

ROUND TOWER CRAB AND CELERIAC REMOULADE

The theories surrounding the purpose of round towers nearly outnumber the surviving towers: places to hide gold, jewel-encrusted chalices and other treasures from Viking robbers; somewhere for people to retreat to when neighbouring tribes of cattle raiders were on the loose; or simply towers built to house a bell to call the un-free Irish workers in from far-flung fields. 'Tall food' built up on the plate to resemble gravity-defying towers is fast going out of fashion, but alternating layers are sometimes a tasty way of mingling flavours and presenting food prettily on the plate. The Irish have no patience with dismantling a whole crab and this recipe, with its unusual but satisfying combination of flavours, makes a tasty, and more importantly, an easy to eat starter.

SERVES 4

Ingredients:

450 g/1 lb white crab meat, fresh or frozen

1 small celeriac

250 ml/8 fl oz/1 cup mayonnaise

1 teasp Irish mustard, or to taste

2 tablesp fresh parsley, finely chopped

juice of half a lemon

half a red pepper, roasted, deseeded and cubed (optional)

Garnish:

oakleaf, cos, endive, water or land cress, and rocket or mizuna, torn into small pieces

wedges of lemon or lime

Method:

If the crab meat is frozen, thaw it fully, then dry thoroughly on absorbent kitchen paper. Mix the mustard and mayonnaise together and stir just enough into the crab meat to achieve a moist but not sloppy consistency. Season with salt and freshly ground black pepper.

Peel and slice the celeriac very thinly horizontally. Blanch in boiling, salted water for a couple of minutes. Drain, cool under running water, then sprinkle with lemon juice. Trim with a large metal scone cutter into circles about 5 cm /3 inches wide.

Assemble by placing a slice of celeriac on a plate, then spoon some crab meat neatly on top and repeat for about three layers. Garnish with cubes of red pepper, parsley, and salad leaves lightly dressed in vinaigrette, or with Cashel Blue cheese dressing (see recipe p.19).

Serve with brown soda bread and butter, or savoury scones.

Round Tower

OYSTERS

The Irish have eaten oysters since the first hunter-gatherers arrivednine thousand years ago; vast mounds of oyster shells have been uncovered in their kitchen middens in estuaries where oysters were plentiful. Native Irish oysters are in season from September to April (when there is an 'r' in the month). Pacific oysters are now cultivated all around our coast and are edible all year round.

Oysters must be tightly shut – any shell that is even slightly open should be thrown away. To prise them open, place them on a work surface with the round side of the shell facing down. Wrap your left hand in a cloth. Place the oyster in your left palm, flat side uppermost. Push the point of the short, blunt oyster knife into the hinge. Press the middle fingers of your left hand on to the shell. Wiggle the knife blade to left and right then (carefully) jerk up the knife to prise the shells apart. Free the oyster from its base and turn its best side up (all the while taking care not to lose any of the delicious juice).

True oyster-lovers spurn any additions at all and eat them straight from the shell, washed down by the juices lingering there. Sometimes a plate of sliced brown soda bread and butter is served, but only to mop up the traditional pint of stout that inevitably and gloriously accompanies the public devouring of oysters (early September in Clarinbridge, just outside Galway town). There's even a very good micro-brewery in Dublin that flavours one of its stouts with oysters. I'm told it's 'magic'. I think I'll take that on trust!

Oysters toughen when cooked and so must be protected from heat. A tasty topping is the only way. The following three are delicious.

OYSTERS ON HORSEBACK

This is a classic.

Take very thin slices of rindless streaky bacon rashers and wrap a slice around each oyster. Grill under a high heat just until the bacon is cooked. Eat at once, they do not keep.

OYSTERS TOPPED WITH HERB/GARLIC BUTTER

Put a coin-sized piece of flavoured butter on top of the oyster and place under a very hot grill only until the butter melts and sizzles. Eat at once.

OYSTERS TOPPED WITH CREAM, BREADCRUMBS AND CHEESE

Dribble a teaspoon of cream over each oyster, then sprinkle with a little grated Gabriel or Parmesan cheese mixed with equal quantities of fine white breadcrumbs, and finish off with a drizzle of melted butter. Place under a very hot grill for about 3 minutes, or until lightly-browned. Eat immediately.

the irish breakfast

'The Full Irish', as it is affectionately known, is not for the faint-hearted. Once it would have been cooked over a turf fire on a great, black, cast-iron frying pan, it is now (except by unreconstructed ex-rugby players) more usually grilled – apart, of course, from the fried egg!

As well as bacon rashers, sausages, slices of black and white pudding and tomatoes, the Irish breakfast can contain mushrooms, potato cake, griddle bread, and in some places, even baked beans. While it would once have been the standard daily breakfast of many, most people nowadays would only eat this as a weekend treat or as a brunch. If what you want is a more manageable meal, rather than cutting out ingredients, serve only one rasher, one sausage, and toasted (instead of fried) bread.

SERVES 4

Ingredients:

4 rashers of back bacon, (rinds snipped with a scissors every 2 cm/1 inch to stop them curling)

4 rashers of streaky bacon, (snipped as above)

8 breakfast sausages

4 tomatoes, halved

4 slices black pudding

4 slices white pudding

4 eggs, fried or poached

4 small slices of bread

or 4 small potato cakes

a little butter or oil

Method:

Grill the tomatoes, sausages and puddings. Start the tomatoes cut side down and half way through cooking turn the cut side up. Sausages and puddings are turned carefully so that they brown on all sides. In a frying pan heat a little bacon fat (or butter, or olive oil). Fry the bread in this until crisp. Lay the rashers on top of the cooked sausages and puddings and grill until the fat is crisp and the meat cooked. Meanwhile add a little more fat to the pan and fry the eggs on one side only, basting occasionally with the fat – these are cooked to taste, but most Irish people like them with the yolk still 'runny'. Serve the rashers, sausages, tomatoes and puddings with the fried eggs (on top of the fried bread) and accompanied by plenty of wholemeal brown bread and butter and a large pot of strong tea.

The Ulster Fry

If The Full Irish is now sometimes grilled, The Ulster Fry, on the other hand, remains defiantly unreconstructed, at least in name, and if you thought The Full Irish was a big breakfast, it's only in the ha'penny place by comparison with the breakfast of our northern relatives!

SERVES 4

Ingredients:

(Rashers, sausages, tomatoes, black and white pudding, eggs, as in *The Full Irish*)

110 g/4 oz mushrooms, preferably large, mature, open-capped mushrooms (or 'flats')

4 potato cakes, **or** small boxty breads

2 farls of griddle bread (see recipe p.88)

Method:

Slice the mushrooms (or leave them whole, but they'll take longer to cook) and pan-fry in very little butter. The mushrooms will absorb the butter and begin to brown, so don't be tempted to add more butter. In another pan fry the potato cakes in butter or bacon fat. Split the farls of griddle bread horizontally and fry them in bacon fat, too.

I did warn you it would 'put hairs on your chest'!

Variation:

When either *The Full Irish* or *The Ulster Fry* is eaten in the afternoon or evening ('breakfast served all day' is a common Irish euphemism for a place where you can cure yourself after a night of over-indulgence in drink) it metamorphoses into 'the mixed grill' in the South, or 'an Irish fry' in the North. Common to both are the extra ingredients: grilled lamb kidneys, slices of pan-fried liver, a lamb chop (if you're lucky) and/or a small piece of steak.

PORRIDGE

In days gone by, breakfast porridge was known as stirabout.

'The children of the lower grade are fed to a bare sufficiency on stirabout made of oatmeal on buttermilk or water, taken with salt butter. The sons of chieftain grades are fed to satiety on stirabout made of barley meal upon new milk, taken with fresh butter. The sons of kings are fed upon stirabout made with wheaten meal upon new milk and taken with honey.'(Excerpt from seventh and eight century Brehon Laws, detailing the feeding regime for foster children).

Long before the arrival of the potato, oats were the Irish winter staple and were used in lots of ways. Whole oats were ground, leaving the groats. When these are chopped into pieces they are called pinhead or coarse oatmeal. These may then be ground into oat flour, or steamed and rolled into oat-flakes. Porridge is made with either pinhead oatmeal or with oat flakes, which (given the advantage of much faster cooking) are more commonly used for making porridge today. Porridge is a simple, nutritious dish, and thanks to the new status of oats as a health food, it's as popular today as ever.

Ingredients:

FOR EACH SERVING

40 g/1 ½oz/½ cup oat flakes

375 ml/1 ½ cups cold water or milk

a pinch of salt

Hob method:

Place oat flakes and liquid in a pot and stir. Bring to boiling point, then simmer for about 6 minutes, stirring regularly. Serve hot with cream and honey, or with a fruit topping.

Microwave method:

Place oat flakes and liquid in a largish bowl and stir. Cook at 600 watts for 3½ minutes or 800 watts for 2½ minutes. Stir halfway through cooking time. Stand for 2 minutes before serving. Note: If cooking double the amount, it will take double the time.

pinhead oatmeal porridge

SERVES 4

Ingredients:

135 g/4¾ oz/1 cup pinhead oatmeal

1 ltr/4 cups water

1 level teasp salt

Method:

Bring the water to the boil in a pot. Slowly sprinkle in the oatmeal, stirring rapidly all the time to prevent lumps. Simmer for 30 minutes, adding salt near the end. Cook until it has reached the consistency you like.

Serve hot with cream or a fruit topping.

fresh herrings in oatmeal

A classic dish. The oatmeal gives a crisp coating and a nutty taste. Traditionally the humble herring languished at the bottom of the fish hierarchy — the fish of the poor, the fish of penitence, a fish that failed to inspire love. Until relatively recent times towns and villages all over the island celebrated 'the whipping of the herring' on the Saturday before Easter to mark the end of the Lenten fast. A herring was threaded onto a rod and a crowd of lads, often the butchers' apprentices, whipped the herring through the streets with long rods. In some towns the final indignity was to drown it! However, in coastal areas, the Irish did eat herring, especially when shoals came near the shore in September. Fresh, they were known as harvest herrings; the surplus was salted and stored in barrels to eat as a 'savour' for potatoes — first soaked in water overnight, then simmered in the pot with the potatoes. In more prosperous households they were 'soused' in beer and vinegar, or given a coating of oatmeal and fried.

SERVES 4

Ingredients:

4-8 very fresh herring fillets*

8 heaped tablesp oat flakes

2 eggs, beaten

3 tablesp plain white flour

4 tablesp butter

* as herrings vary so much in size you will have to be the judge of how many you will need from the fish available on the day.

Method:

Wash and dry the fish. Dip each one in flour first, then in egg, then in oat flakes (press the latter on to the fish). If you have time, rest in a cool place to allow this coating to set. Heat a large frying pan, add some of the butter and heat it until it begins to foam. Add the herrings and cook on one side until the oat flakes are evenly browned but not burnt. Turn with a fish slice, add extra butter if needed, and brown on the second side. If you need to cook in batches, keep the first batch warm.

Serve with wedges of lemon and grilled tomato halves.

WOODCOCK SMOKERY KIPPERS WITH POTATO SALAD AND POACHED EGG

This recipe is by Ross Lewis of Chapter One restaurant in Dublin. It was prepared for the luncheon at which the Irish Food Writers Guild announced their Food Award winners for 2001. Sally Barnes's Woodcock Smokery kippers won an award and are spectacularly good.

SERVES 4

Ingredients:

6 baby waxy potatoes, such as Nicola or Charlotte

a little white wine vinegar

4 small eggs

4 Woodcock Smokery kippers

15 g/½ oz/1 tablesp unsalted butter

a little olive oil

1 tablesp snipped fresh chives

4 fresh chervil sprigs

For the mustard beurre blanc:

125 ml/4 fl oz/½ cup tarragon vinegar

60 ml/2 fl oz/¼ cup dry white wine

2 shallots, very finely chopped

60 ml/2 fl oz/¼ cup double cream

135 g/4½ oz/1 (very generous) stick unsalted butter, chilled and diced

1 tablesp wholegrain mustard

½ tablesp Dijon mustard

Maldon sea salt and freshly ground black pepper

Method:

Preheat the oven to 220°C/450°F/Gas 7, or the grill to high. Place the potatoes in a pan of boiling salted water, cover and bring to the boil. Reduce the heat and simmer for 15-20 minutes until tender. Drain and leave to cool a little, then carefully peel away the skins and cut each potato into 2 even-sized rounds, discarding the rounded ends.

Heat a large deep pan two-thirds full with water and add one tablespoon of vinegar for each 1.2 litres/2 pints/1¼ US quarts of water. Bring to the boil and then break the eggs one at a time into where the water is bubbling. Reduce the heat and simmer gently for 3 minutes, then carefully remove the eggs with a slotted spoon into a large bowl of iced water to prevent further cooking. When cold, trim any ragged ends from the cooked egg whites.

To make the mustard *beurre blanc*, place the vinegar, wine and shallots in a small pan and reduce to 2 tablespoons. Stir in the cream. Reduce the heat to very low, whisk in the butter cubes, a few at a time, adding the next batch just before the butter already in the pan is entirely melted, whisking all the time. Stir in both mustards and season to taste. Keep warm over a very, very low heat.

Arrange the kippers on a baking sheet and dot with butter. Place in the oven or under the grill for 2-3 minutes until warm, then remove the skin. Keep warm. Heat the olive oil in a sauté pan, add the potato rounds, season and just warm through, tossing occasionally. Place the poached eggs in a pan of gently simmering salted water for 1 minute to heat through.

To serve, arrange three pieces of potato on each serving plate and add the kippers. Place the poached eggs on top and cover with the mustard *beurre blanc*. Season to taste and scatter over the chives, then garnish with the chervil sprigs.

GRILLED MACKEREL AND GOOSEBERRY SAUCE

Mackerel is an oily fish. It is traditionally served with a sauce that 'cuts' the fat – gooseberry is in season at the time mackerel shoal off our coasts and so is the most usual accompaniment. Mackerel must be eaten very fresh – preferably cooked the moment it is removed from the hook! While the Japanese eat mackerel raw, in Ireland we prefer it either fried or spit-roasted straight out of the sea, or filleted and hot-smoked, then either made into a creamed pâté, or served with a creamed horseradish sauce.

SERVES 4

Ingredients:

4 fresh mackerel, filleted and pin-bones carefully removed

a little melted butter **or** olive oil

450 g/1 lb green gooseberries

3 tablesp dry white wine **or** water

2 tablesp sugar

1 tablesp butter

2 teasp fresh ginger, peeled, shredded, and finely chopped

sea salt and freshly ground black pepper

Method:

Top, tail, and wash the gooseberries. Heat the sugar and water together until the sugar has dissolved. Add the gooseberries, ginger and wine and cook gently until tender. Stir in the butter and serve as it is, hot (purée, if you prefer).

Brush the mackerel with butter or oil, season with freshly ground pepper and sea salt, and grill for about 4 minutes on each side – keep checking, mackerel is best ever-so-slightly undercooked in the centre.

Variations:

Stuff each fish with one teaspoon of Florence fennel flesh (or leaves, to taste) very finely chopped.

Stuff each fish with chopped mushroom cooked in butter and flavoured with chopped parsley and a very small amount of chopped fresh sage.

PAN-FRIED TROUT

Our native brown trout, caught in rivers, are loved by fishermen, if for no other reason than they fight hardest. Brown trout and white (sea) trout are twins. But the white trout has changed its lifestyle by going out to sea and only re-entering the rivers to spawn, in the same way as salmon (causing it to be called 'salmon trout' by some people). In recent years white trout have become increasingly scarce. Rainbow trout originated in America and are farmed extensively. Fed so that that their flesh becomes pink like 'white' trout, they are the least expensive and most widely available fish on sale.

From a cook's point of view these fish are interchangeable but, it has to be said, a fresh brown trout or a white trout needs very little 'tarting up', while the flabbier farmed trout benefits from it.

SERVES 4

Ingredients:

4 trout fillets or 4 cleaned trout on the bone

2 tablesp olive oil, or butter and oil mixed

4 whole sprigs (or freshly chopped) fresh dill weed

salt and freshly ground black pepper

Method:

Whole trout should be lightly scored on each side. Heat the oil – or the oil and butter – in a large non-stick pan. Season the fish with salt and freshly ground black pepper and pan-fry, turning just once, for 3-5 minutes each side or until just done. Place a whole sprig of dill inside each whole fish, or scatter chopped dill over the fillets during cooking. Do not overcook; time depends on size and whether the fish is whole or filleted. It should still be juicy and not quite cooked right through to the bone.

Serve at once.

BALLYNAHINCH PAN-FRIED TOURNEDOS OF WILD SALMON

WITH BUTTERED CABBAGE, SMOKED BACON AND TRUMPET MUSHROOMS, AND A BEURRE BLANC SAUCE

Wild Irish salmon is in season from January to September. Ballynahinch Castle Hotel, Connemara, County Galway, owns the fishing rights to one of the finest salmon rivers in Ireland. The hotel's head chef is tested more than most (having to come up with a such a variety of delicious ways of cooking salmon). This unusual combination is not difficult to cook if you have all the ingredients to hand.

SERVES 4

Ingredients:

4 salmon portions, about 200 g/7 oz in weight, boned

a little clarified butter

225 g/8 oz green cabbage leaves, blanched and shredded

110g /4 oz smoked bacon, finely chopped

6 dried black trumpet mushrooms (*trompets des morts*), completely reconstituted in very hot water, then dried

a little more clarified butter

Garnish:

cooked baby potatoes, cooked asparagus tips, and *beurre blanc* sauce

Season salmon with salt and pepper. Heat a pan, melt clarified butter and pan-fry the salmon until just done (5-6 minutes depending on thickness). Take care not to overcook.

Heat another pan, add a knob of butter and then the bacon and mushrooms. When the bacon is cooked, add the cabbage and cook, stirring, until hot through. Season to taste with salt and black pepper.

Place the cabbage in the centre of the plate, set the salmon on top, and surround with the garnishes and a *beurre blanc* sauce.

whole poached salmon

Almost mandatory on an Irish buffet table, this is usually served very decoratively, with its skin and scales replaced by very finely sliced cucumber slices (time-consuming, but undoubtedly charming to look at).

SERVES 10-20 depending on weight of fish

Method:

Take one whole salmon. Lay the fish on its side in a fish kettle (on a strip of foil or muslin to enable you to lift it out easily). Pour over just enough water or vegetable stock (add a little drinkable dry white wine, if you like) to barely cover. Over a low heat bring it slowly to a bare simmer. Then, if the fish is to be eaten cold, turn off the heat and let the fish cool in the liquid before lifting it out. Before it is completely cold, skin it by slitting the skin along the back and peeling it away.

If the fish is to be eaten hot, continue simmering for 10 minutes for the first kilo/2¼ lb, 15 minutes for the second, and 20 minutes for the third. The flesh should be just opaque at the bone and you should be able to easily push a thin skewer into the thickest part of the fish.

seared scallops with nut-brown butter and lemon juice

Scallops are common all around the Irish coast, the larger ones are more plentiful and the smaller Queens considered a treat simply because they are seen less often. Woe betide the cook who removes the orange roe from either variety! Being an expensive treat they are most often eaten as a starter.

SERVES 4

Ingredients:

8 large scallops, **or** 12 Queens

2 tablesp fresh parsley, chopped

175 g/6 oz/1½ sticks butter

juice of half a lemon

Garnishes:

Chefs get creative with scallops because they go well with any number of garnishes. Indulge your tastes as long as you remember that a scallop is very delicate in flavour and easily overwhelmed.

A few compatible ideas:

Instead of parsley use a few slivers of finely sliced scallions (green onions), or scatter some chopped chives on top.

In addition to the parsley, add a couple of tablespoons of slivered bacon rasher, grilled until crisp.

As an alternative to the browned butter, use a citrus vinaigrette: 6 tablesp olive oil whisked with 2 tablesp orange juice, 1 tablesp lemon juice, seasoned with salt and pepper.

Method:

Clean the scallops, removing the muscular white frill opposite the roe. Rinse under running water and dry. Queens are cooked whole; large scallops may be halved horizontally.

To make the browned butter: chop butter into small pieces and heat it in a pan over a medium flame until it just begins to brown – you will know it's done when a delicate, nutty aroma wafts from the pan. Keep the butter warm and have warm plates at the ready.

Heat a non-stick pan, very lightly greased with a little light olive oil, and sear the scallops for 30 seconds on each side. Do not overcook or they will become tough. Remove at once from the pan. They will hold for a minute if placed on greaseproof paper in a warm place. Place on serving plates, squeeze a little lemon juice on top, season with sea salt and freshly ground black pepper, then pour the brown butter over and scatter with parsley.

Serve with fresh crusty soda (or yeast) bread to mop up the juices.

Scallop

DUBLIN BAY PRAWNS

WITH LEMON JUICE, BUTTER AND GARLIC

A marine creature whose common name seems to confuse everyone except the Irish! They are not caught not in Dublin Bay at all but in Atlantic waters. Long ago, fishing boats coming into Dublin port sold them direct to barrow vendors. Nephrops are the same creature as Norway lobster, Italian scampi, French langoustine, and American shrimp! Everyone clear now?

SERVES 4

Ingredients:

1 kg/2¼ lbs (at least) prawns in the shell

60 g/2 oz/½ stick butter

1 tablesp olive oil

2 lemons (the juice of 1 lemon, the other cut into quarters lengthways)

2 tablesp chopped parsley

1 clove of garlic, peeled, crushed and chopped (optional)

Method:

Heat the pan, add butter and oil, then stir-fry the prawns for 3–4 minutes. Add lemon juice, garlic and parsley. Tip onto a hot platter and serve with lemon wedges, brown bread and butter – and lots of paper napkins.

Variations:

Peel prawns after cooking and serve with a homemade or high quality bought mayonnaise (do resist the temptation to flavour this with dollops of tomato ketchup!) and a wedge of lemon.

Peel prawns before cooking and, using either a batter or a breadcrumb coating, deep-fry them for serving as scampi served with wedges of lemon and mayonnaise.

Peel prawns before cooking, wrap in filo (phyllo) pastry, and deep-fry. Serve with a spicy chilli jam or a salsa.

Cook's Tip:

Peeling and Cooking Prawns

Rinse the prawns. Pull off the legs (keep to make stock). The prawns are always best cooked in the shell – and lightly cooked at that! Boil in salted water for 2 minutes after the water comes back to the boil; steam for 3 minutes; or stir-fry for 3–4 minutes. Prawns are peeled by holding the 'head' where it joins the tail, gently squeezing the body and peeling away the shell (from the underside). The body, or tail, is slipped out with a gentle tug. Most people prefer to remove the thin, black thread (the intestine).

If frozen raw prawns are used they must be thawed slowly and fully in a glass or china dish, drained, then washed and dried. Frozen cooked prawns must be thawed slowly, dried thoroughly on absorbent kitchen paper, and are then ready to eat.

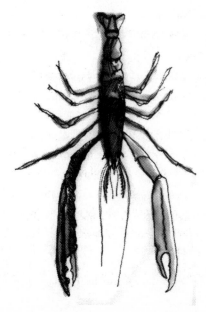

ÐUBLIN CODDLE

Said to have been a favourite dish of Jonathan Swift, Dean of St Patrick's Cathedral and author of the famous Gulliver's Travels, *this dish is now rarely eaten outside Dublin. In the area of the inner city known as the Liberties it is a favourite Saturday night dish and also a funeral food – a humbler version of 'baked, funeral meats'. The reason is purely practical – it doesn't spoil if left cooking for an extra hour or two.*

SERVES 4–6

Ingredients:

450 g/1 lb bacon bits*, **or** a streaky bacon joint, cubed

450 g/1 lb good quality (meaty) Irish breakfast sausages

3 large onions, peeled, and chopped

1¼ kg/3 lb floury potatoes, peeled

6 tablesp fresh parsley, chopped

freshly ground black pepper to taste

500 ml/16 fl oz/2 cups water

*Bacon 'bits' are off-cuts from various types of bacon (both smoked and pale) and are sold cheaply in Dublin pork butchers' shops specially for coddle. Normally they contain a fairly even mixture of fat and lean. Streaky bacon also works well; keep the skin on for more flavour.

Method:

Cut the potatoes into fairly large pieces (leave them whole if small). Chop the fresh parsley. Choose a heavy pot with a really tight-fitting lid. Put a generous layer of chopped onions on the bottom and then layer the other ingredients, giving each layer a generous twist of pepper. Bring to the boil, then reduce the heat to a bare simmer. Cover very tightly. Cook for 2–5 hours! The longer and slower the cooking, the better this dish will be. It cannot come to any harm

providing the lid is really tight. A very low oven is best, set at
120°C/250°F/Gas ½.

In some homes, what my son once christened 'slithery' (boiled and not
browned) sausages are disliked. You can either lay all the sausages on top and,
just before serving, set the pot under a grill to brown them. Even better,
remove the sausages to brown under a hot grill just before serving, although
this will probably be anathema to the coddle purists!

Dublin Coddle is traditionally served with buttered white soda bread and
bottles of stout. You can also serve it with quickly-cooked green cabbage.

St Patrick's Cathedral, Dublin.

CORNED BEEF

Until relatively recent times most Irish beef was exported, much of it 'on the hoof', but a great deal salted in barrels – corned beef, as we know it. This would have been the only beef that ordinary Irish people ever ate; on some feast days like Christmas a farmer might slaughter an elderly cow (one past breeding or milking) and send out a cut to his neighbours – the beef equivalent of 'the Christmas pudding round'. Corned beef is mentioned in the eleventh century dream poem Aishlinge Meic ConGlinne:

> 'Many wonderful provisions, Pieces of palatable food
> Full without fault, Perpetual joints of corned beef.'

Colcannon is the perfect accompaniment for corned beef. Traditional sauces to accompany corned (or spiced) beef and colcannon are a simple white parsley sauce or a mustard sauce.

SERVES 4–6

Ingredients:

1¼ kg/3 lb (approx) corned beef (silverside, topside, round, rump – **or** brisket which is much fattier)

1 onion

1 carrot

bouquet garni

2 cloves garlic

500 ml/1 pt/2 cups/(small bottle) dry cider

Method:

Soak the meat overnight in several changes of water. Place all the ingredients in a large ovenproof pot with fresh water to cover. Bring to the boil, skimming all the while. Reduce heat to a bare simmer and cover tightly. Cooked in the oven at 150°C/300°F/Gas 2, it takes between 40 to 60 minutes per 450 g/1 lb. Tenderness varies (depending on beast, cut and cure), so test when three-quarters of the cooking time has elapsed. If you intend to eat the meat cold, as many Irish prefer, allow it to cool in the cooking water, then remove to a plate and press lightly, either in a meat press, or by covering with a plate weighed down by 2 x 400g food tins.

spiced beef

Spices have been imported into Ireland since earliest times, but were always scarce and expensive, so this dish was one reserved for a festive feast, particularly at Christmas. It's a tradition that lives on today and no Christmas cold table is complete without it. Dry-spicing is the older, more interesting way of curing it but, it has to be said, wet spicing has its fans – some people even defend the modern butchers' method of 'spicing-up' corned beef which, although good to eat if you choose your butcher carefully, is not really the same at all. Do weigh the ingredients for this recipe carefully.

SERVES 6–10

Ingredients for Spicing:

about 2 kg/4½ lb beef (silverside, topside, round, rump, **or** brisket)

15 g/½ oz saltpetre

225 g/8 oz sea salt

30 g/1 oz allspice

30 g/1 oz whole black peppercorns

90 g/3 oz dark brown sugar

12 dried juniper berries (crushed)

a big pinch of ground cloves

2 bay leaves

Ingredients for Cooking:

bunch of thyme

bay leaves

1 onion, studded with cloves

1 carrot

1 stick celery

12 whole peppercorns

Method:

Mix the salt and saltpetre and rub some of it into the meat, making sure it gets well into all the hollows and cracks. Place in a glass or other non-metal bowl and keep covered in the fridge or another really cool place. Repeat this procedure every day for 4 days. Then grind the whole spices and mix them with the sugar, cloves, and bay leaves. Rub this mixture into the beef and place in a clean dish. Store in the fridge. Every second day for 10-14 days, turn the joint over and rub in the spices that adhere to the meat.

To Cook:

Tie a bunch of thyme and a few bay leaves to the joint. Place it in a pot just large enough to fit the meat. Add an onion stuck with a few cloves, a carrot, a stick of celery and a dozen whole peppercorns. Cover with cold water (mixed, if you wish, with a bottle of stout for a distinctive flavour). Bring to simmering point, cover tightly, and cook in a low oven set to 140°C/275°F/Gas 1 for about 5 hours. If you prefer, simmer it gently for about 3½ hours on the hob. It should be quite soft and tender when fully cooked.

Spiced beef can be eaten hot but it is more usual to serve it cold. To do this, allow it to cool in the cooking liquid for about 2 hours, then remove it, wrap in greaseproof paper, and press it lightly while stored in the fridge. Slice very thinly with a very sharp knife. It is often served as finger food on brown bread spread with a fruit chutney; with chopped pickles (sweet and sour pears, sweet pickled onions, or piccalilli are good), or as a plated dish with a green salad, or a celery and walnut salad, and crusty white bread and butter.

ROAST RACK OF LAMB

Irish lamb is famous the world over for its succulent texture and complex flavour –
the happy result of Irish geography and climate. Irish lamb is reared all year round
on the hills that surround the flatter midlands, hills on which hundreds of different
grasses and herbs have grown naturally and in great abundance for centuries. On
the much higher ground of Wicklow, Connemara, and Kerry, mountain lambs
chosen for their ability to withstand colder temperatures grow more slowly and,
although there is a higher proportion of bone to flesh, the meat is sweeter and even
more complex. Mountain lamb comes into season early in the autumn.

SERVES 3–4

Ingredients:

**a rack of lamb, trimmed and
chined**

**2 cloves garlic, peeled and
cut into thin slivers**

**small sprigs of fresh
rosemary**

a little white flour

Method:

Scrape the tips of the lamb bones clean
(about 2.5cm/1 inch) and protect them with
foil. Season the meat and insert slivers of
garlic and sprigs of rosemary between each
chop (cutlet). Sprinkle flour on the fat side –
this helps crisp the fat. Place on a rack in a
roasting tin in an oven preheated to
200°C/400°F/Gas 6. Roast for 30-35 minutes
(for fairly pink lamb). Carve 2-3 cutlets per
person and serve at once.

Variations:

Serve with wine and rosemary *jus*. Simmer
½ cup red wine with 1½ cups lamb stock and
1 tablesp chopped fresh rosemary leaves until
reduced by one third. Strain. Reheat to
boiling point and whisk in 4 tablesp of
chilled, cubed butter, a little at a time. Serve
at once.

IRISh STEW

A simple 'white' stew that's as good as the ingredients from which it is made. Originally made with wild kid (goat), then with mutton, and now, because we cannot easily buy either, with lamb.

Ambitious home cooks and famous chefs produce many complicated variations on this very simple dish, adding everything but the kitchen sink – carrots, celery, turnips, leeks, cabbage, black pudding, cream, and their own restaurant 'stock'. Some of these gourmet Irish stews can be lovely to eat but they are not, in my humble opinion, Irish stew. In its simplest form, Irish stew is the comfort food of the Irish nation. Put a plain, straightforward Irish stew in front of any Irishman (Unionist or Republican) and he'll devour it without fear or favour.

SERVES 4

Ingredients:

1.4 kg/3 lb potatoes, peeled

900 g/2 lb stewing lamb (gigot)

450 g/1 lb onions, chopped

5 tablesp fresh parsley, chopped

1 tablesp fresh thyme, chopped

250-500 ml/8-16 fl oz/1-2 cups of water

salt and freshly ground black pepper

Method:

Peel the potatoes. Leave them whole unless very large. The bones in the meat and a certain amount of fat are essential to the flavour of Irish stew as the potatoes absorb a good deal of the fat and flavour of the meat. The meat is not cubed but left in fairly large pieces. When the meat is cooked enough it falls way from the bone, which then poses no hazard on the plate.

Place a layer of onion on the bottom of a heavy pot or casserole. Lay the meat on this. Season with salt and freshly ground black pepper and sprinkle generously with fresh chopped parsley and much less generously with chopped thyme. Layer the rest of the onions with the potatoes and finish with the rest of the herbs. The amount of water required depends on how good the seal is between pot and lid. Bring to the boil and cover tightly. You may either simmer gently on the hob or cook in the oven at 150°C/300°F/Gas 2 for 2½–3 hours. The finished stew should be moist but definitely not 'swimming' in liquid. Add a little hot water during cooking only if it appears to be getting too dry for your taste. Floury potatoes will partly dissolve into the liquid, thickening it a little, waxy potatoes will not. It's a matter of taste which type you use – I use some of both.

Serve with lots of chopped parsley. Carrots, which should be cooked separately and never in the stew, are the perfect accompaniment.

BEEF STEW

In Ireland beef stews often contain stout or ale instead of, or as well as, stock or water. Which one the cook used would have been entirely dependent upon whether the brewery nearest to home made stout or beer. Like all Irish stews it is eaten with mounds of floury potatoes, but it is also quite common for the potatoes to be cooked (added towards the end of the cooking time) in the pot with the stew. In Dublin the preferred cut of meat would be shin beef because, when given long, slow cooking (a very gentle baking or simmering only), it softens to a melting tenderness and produces thick, rich, gelatinous gravy.

SERVES 4

Ingredients:

450–700 g/1 lb–1½ lb shin beef

2 large onions, peeled and chopped

2–3 carrots, peeled and sliced

30 g/1 oz/2 tablesp butter or beef dripping

pot herbs (bay, parsley, thyme)

225 ml/8 fl oz/1 cup stout or beer

225 ml/8 fl oz/1 cup water

salt and freshly ground black pepper

Method:

Melt the fat in a large frying pan and fry the onions gently until translucent and beginning to brown at the edges. Remove them with a slotted spoon and place them with the sliced carrots in the bottom of a casserole. Remove the outer membrane from the shin beef and any large sinews and gristle. Cut the meat into rounds about 2 cm/1 inch thick and brown them quickly in the hot fat to seal them. Remove the meat from the pan and put in the casserole on top of the carrots and onions. De-glaze the frying pan with the stout or beer. Add this liquid to the casserole along with the water, pot herbs, and seasoning. Cover tightly and cook slowly in a pre-heated oven at 160°C/325°F/Gas 3 for 3 hours.

Like all Irish stews, this is a flexible dish, capable of much embellishment. You may need to thicken the gravy with flour if you use a cut other than shin beef and this should be done by dusting the meat pieces in seasoned flour before sealing it in the frying pan. It can be further enriched by the addition of ox or lamb's kidney.

This stew definitely improves in flavour if allowed to cool before being refrigerated and reheated after a day or two.

MEDALLIONS OF VENISON WITH PORT AND ORANGE SAUCE

Wild venison is plentiful in season and farmed venison is available most of the year. Wild deer have a more complex and variable flavour from grazing diverse and naturally organic land. A haunch, or a saddle, of venison is almost as easy to roast as a leg or a rack of lamb. Being very lean meat, all but the very youngest (tenderest) venison benefits from a day in a simple marinade – of lemon juice, olive oil, garlic and crushed juniper berries, or even with two glasses of a robust red wine added. This recipe is from Martin Dwyer of Dwyer's Restaurant, Waterford – noted for its peaceful atmosphere and for Martin's individual approach to cooking good food in season.

SERVES 4

Ingredients:

1.4 kg/3 lb loin of venison, or 8 ready-prepared medallions

½ bottle of port

1 tablesp redcurrant jelly

juice and zest of 1 large orange

110 g/4 oz/1 stick butter

Method:

Get the butcher to bone the loin so that you are left with a lean fillet (the bones and flap could be used to make a game stock). Cut the fillet into 8 even-sized pieces. Plump them up with your fingers to make them as thick as possible and season well.

Prepare the sauce by boiling down the port until reduced by half. Add the orange juice, zest and redcurrant jelly and simmer for 5 minutes.

Sear the venison on both sides in a hot pan, using half the butter. Cook for a little longer, making sure they are still rare (or at least pink) when you take them up. Keep warm while you finish the sauce. Whisk the remaining butter into the simmering sauce. At Dwyer's the dish is served on a bed of puréed celeriac with the sauce spooned around.

BAKED HAM WITH CIDER, MUSTARD & APPLE SAUCE

Bacon or ham, either pale or smoked, is still much cooked in Irish homes and restaurants and is a special favourite at Christmas. Whole ham weighs 8-11 lbs and serves 14-16 people. A half ham from the fillet end weighs 4-5½ lbs and serves 6-10. A ham from the hock end contains more bone and sinew and serves 4-8 max.

Ingredients:

1 joint of ham

1 onion, peeled

1 carrot

1 celery stalk

1 bay leaf

8 whole black peppercorns

For the glaze:

12 whole cloves

250 ml/8 fl oz/1 cup freshly squeezed orange juice

2-3 tablesp Demerara sugar

1 teasp English mustard powder

For the sauce:

1 Bramley cooking apple, peeled, cored and chopped

1 teasp sugar, or to taste

1 tablesp wholegrain Irish mustard

2 teasp butter

Method

Soak joint for 12 hours in two changes of water. Place in a large pot, add vegetables, bay leaf and peppercorns and cover with cold water. Bring slowly to simmering point, cover and barely simmer for 25 minutes for each 450 g/1 lb (for joints over 3.5 kg/8 lb, allow 20 minutes per 450 g/1 lb). Leave to cool a little in its cooking liquid off the heat. Lift out and remove the skin, leaving the fat. Mix sugar and dry mustard powder and press evenly all over the joint. With a sharp knife cut a lattice pattern in the fat. Press back any coating that falls off. Stick a clove into the cuts where the lines cross. Heat oven to 220°C/425°F/Gas 7. Place the ham in a roasting tin surrounded by the orange juice. Bake for about 20 minutes or until the sugar has slightly caramelised.

Cook the apple in the cider and sugar until soft. Beat with a wooden spoon until smooth. Stir in the mustard and butter and season to taste.

COLCANNON

For a dish that is not widely eaten today, colcannon remains remarkably widely known. And it has the distinction of having a song dedicated to it, a song that, like the recipe itself, has two versions. If you say 'colcannon' in a crowded room, chances are that half the room will break into one version of the song and the other half into a completely different version.

COLCANNON MADE WITH KALE:

'Did you ever eat colcannon when 'twas made with yellow cream
And the kale and praties blended like the picture in a dream?
Did you ever take a forkful and dip it in the lake
Of heather-flavoured butter that your mother used to make?
Oh you did, yes you did! So did he and so did I,
And the more I think about it sure, the more I want to cry.'

COLCANNON MADE WITH CABBAGE:

'Did you ever eat colcannon when 'twas made with thickened cream
And the greens and scallions blended like the picture in a dream?
Did you ever scoop a hole on top to hold the melting cake
Of clover-flavoured butter which your mother used to make?
Did you ever eat and eat, afraid you'd let the ring go past,
And some old married sprissman would get it at the last?'

BOTH VERSIONS END WITH:

'God be with the happy times when trouble we had not
And our mothers made colcannon in the little three-legged pot.'

Colcannon is so like champ, cally, stampy and poundies that it is difficult to understand how it ever came to have a different name. Yet, all over the country, colcannon is colcannon and known as nothing else. As in the two versions of the song, it can be made with kale or with greens – meaning cabbage. Those reared on the version made with kale don't accept the cabbage version as colcannon and those in the other camp, I'm sure, are equally insistent that their method is the true one. I was reared without the addition of scallions and feel that they interfere with the very individual taste of kale. Others would maintain that they are an essential ingredient.

Colcannon is eaten at Hallowe'en when the kale crop is ready, and often had a ring put into it as a 'favour' – a tradition taken over by barm brack in most parts of Ireland today.

SERVES 6–8

Ingredients:

1 kg/2½ lb floury potatoes, peeled

250 ml/8 fl oz/1 cup curly kale* leaves, cooked and finely chopped

250 ml/8 fl oz/1 cup hot milk

1 bunch (about 6) scallions, finely chopped (optional)

4 tablesp butter

salt and freshly ground black pepper

*For 'Cabbage Colcannon' omit the kale and substitute 250 ml/8 fl oz/1 cup finely chopped green cabbage

Method:

Steam the potatoes until tender. Dry off by placing a clean tea-towel on top for a few minutes. Then put through a potato ricer or mouli.

Strip the soft kale leaf away from the stem and tougher veins. Discard the stem and veins. Shred the leaves finely. Bring a large, stainless-steel pot of salted water to a furious boil, add the kale leaves and cook until just tender. Drain and cool immediately under cold running water – vital if you wish to preserve its bright green colour. Drain, then squeeze out any excess liquid. Place the kale in a food processor with the hot milk and process until you have a thick green 'soup'.

Put the scallions (if using) in a small pan with the butter and soften for just 30 seconds.

Lightly, but thoroughly, mix the scallions, potatoes and kale until you have a pale green fluff. Season with salt and freshly ground black pepper, then reheat until piping hot in the microwave or (covered) in an oven. Serve with more butter.

champ

'There was an old woman who lived in a lamp,

She had no room to beetle her champ.

She ups with the beetle and broke the lamp,

And then she had room to beetle her champ.'

'Poundies', 'stampy' and 'cally' are all variations of this dish composed of mashed, floury potatoes to which various vegetables are added. The beetle or poundy was the wooden implement with which the potatoes were 'beetled' or 'pounded' – they ate seriously large amounts of potato in those days! Historically the commonest recipe used onions of whatever kind was available. Today, scallions (spring, or green, onions) are most often used, but chives are also used in restaurants.

SERVES 4

Ingredients:

900 g/2 lb floury potatoes

1 large bunch scallions (about one cup) chopped

250 ml/8 fl oz/1 cup milk

butter to taste

salt and freshly ground black pepper

Method:

Steam the potatoes (preferably in their skins). Dry using an absorbent cloth or tea towel, then peel. Chop the scallions and simmer in the milk for just a minute or two. Keep warm. Put the potatoes through a potato ricer or mouli, or mash thoroughly. Add the milk and scallion mixture and mix through lightly. You may add more milk if the mixture seems dry, but on no account should it become wet. Reheat until piping hot. Place each serving on a very hot plate, and then make 'a dunt' (depression) in the centre. Place a good knob of butter into this and allow it to melt into a little lake. Eat from the outside in, dipping each forkful into the butter.

Variations:

Substitute 1 cup of cooked peas or finely chopped, young, skinned broad beans for the scallions; or add cooked chopped onion, cooked mashed parsnip, or cooked mashed turnip (swede), or finely chopped young nettle tops (cooked in the milk until tender). Chives, parsley, or wild garlic (finely chopped) are added directly to the potato rather than cooked in the milk first.

"beetle"

celeriac and potato purée

Celeriac is a root vegetable with a high water content and makes for a softer, wetter purée than traditional champ dishes. Its knobbly appearance puts off many people, but the flavour, which is similar to celery, makes it an especially good accompaniment to game.

SERVES 4–6

Ingredients:

450 g/1 lb floury potatoes, peeled

900 g/2 lb celeriac (weighed after peeling)

60 g/2 oz/½ stick butter

60 ml/2 fl oz/¼ cup cream

Method:

Steam the potatoes until tender. Dry; then put them through a potato ricer or mouli. Cut the celeriac into large chunks and boil in salted water until tender. Dry them off before puréeing in a food processor. Combine the two vegetables then add butter and cream; season to taste, and mix well. Serve very hot.

Celeriac

potato and chestnut purée

Good with goose, duck and game birds like pheasant and wild duck. Chestnuts
(being very troublesome to prepare) are usually bought ready-cooked and peeled.
Excellent French, or Italian cooked, peeled, whole chestnuts (marrons or marroni)
can be bought shrink-wrapped in good speciality shops. Tinned cooked ones are
available in most supermarkets. Dried chestnuts are not as succulent; they can be
reconstituted by soaking overnight and boiling for 30 minutes. The sweet chestnut is
completely unrelated to the inedible horse chestnut, Aesculus hippocastum,
which grows plentifully in Ireland and provides the conkers that little boys are so
fond of.

SERVES 4

Ingredients:

**450 g/1 lb floury potatoes
peeled**

**400 g/14 oz/2 cups whole,
cooked chestnuts (weighed
when cooked and peeled)**

90 g/3 oz/³/₄ stick butter

60 ml/2 fl oz/¼ cup cream

Method:

Steam the potatoes until tender; dry, then put
through a potato ricer or mouli. Purée the
cooked chestnuts with the cream in a food
processor. Mix with the potatoes and butter.
Season to taste and serve very hot.

Chestnuts

chapter one champ

This is a luxury champ by Ross Lewis, head chef at Chapter One Restaurant in Dublin.

SERVES 4

Ingredients:

4 large organic Rooster potatoes

225 ml/8 fl oz/1 cup cream

110 g/4 oz/1 stick butter

4 scallions, chopped

Maldon sea salt

freshly ground black pepper

Method:

Steam or boil the potatoes in their skins; peel them and pass through a mouli or potato ricer. Reduce the cream and butter by half in a pot. Stir in the scallions. Dry off the potatoes in a heavy pan, then add the cream and butter mixture. Season with crushed Maldon sea salt and freshly ground black pepper.

hallowe'en pudding

This pudding is eaten at Hallowe'en in the Lower Ards area of Ulster. It could also make a lighter alternative to traditional Christmas pudding. 'Favours', which always include a ring – often a brass curtain ring – are placed in the pudding at Hallowe'en (for safety wrap these in greaseproof paper).

SERVES 4–6

Ingredients

60 g/2 oz/ ½ cup white flour

90 g/3 oz/¾ stick butter, cut into small dice

110 g/4 oz/1 cup wholemeal breadcrumbs

½ teasp bicarbonate of soda

1 teasp mixed spice/allspice

½ teasp salt

60 g/2 oz/¼ cup caster sugar

250 g/8 oz/1¼ cups mixed dried fruit

1 tablesp treacle/molasses

175 ml/6 fl oz/¾ cup buttermilk

Method:

Sift the flour and place in a mixing bowl with the butter. Rub the butter into the flour until the mixture resembles breadcrumbs. Sift the soda, mixed spice and salt together and mix thoroughly into the flour mixture Add all the other ingredients, using just enough buttermilk to give a soft but not sloppy mixture. Grease a 1 ltr/2 lb/2 pt pudding bowl with butter (it needs to be large enough to allow the mixture to expand). Cover with a double thickness of greaseproof paper, making a pleat in the middle. Tie tightly with string, looping it across the centre to make a handle with which to lift the cooked pudding from the pot. Steam for about 3 hours.

Serve hot with whipped, fresh cream or an egg custard sauce (see recipe p. 63).

EGG CUSTARD SAUCE

Good with many puddings, dumplings, fruit pies and tarts. Custard is a mixture of milk and eggs thickened by heating. It has been used since medieval times. In the nineteenth century, Alfred Bird, an experimental chemist, invented the commercial custard powder, which is not a dried form of custard, but consists mainly of cornflour, sugar and milk solids. Bird came up with the concoction because his wife liked custard but was allergic to eggs. So successful was he that his invention has all but supplanted egg custard. However, for texture and flavour there is nothing to beat the real thing.

Ingredients:

250 ml/8 fl oz/1 US cup full-fat milk

1 vanilla pod, or cinnamon stick, or the finely grated zest of one orange

2 egg yolks

60 g/2 oz/(scant) ¼ cup caster sugar

Method:

Put the vanilla pod and milk in a saucepan and bring close to simmering point. Remove from heat and allow to infuse for 10 minutes. Blend egg yolks and sugar in the top pot of a double saucepan. Whisk in the warm milk and sit the pot on the lower pot of hot (but not boiling) water. Cook gently, stirring or whisking continuously, until the sauce is creamy and coats the back of a wooden spoon.

Serve at once. If you need to keep the sauce warm for a while, place the serving-jug in a pot of warm (but not hot) water.

Cook's Tip

If, due to excessive heat, the sauce curdles, pour it immediately into a cold bowl and whisk furiously.

chRistMas puddiNG

Christmas pudding was first served, as far as written accounts record, to William the Conqueror by his chef Robert Argyllion on the occasion of his coronation in 1066. No doubt it came to Ireland by way of our own Norman conquerors. It's a dish that has taken many twists and turns down the years: once it was a kind of meat stew, by Elizabethan times it had become a meat porridge sweetened with fruit, a century later it had solidified into the dark, rich pudding we know today.

MAKES 5 x 450 g/1lb puddings or about 20 individual puddings

Ingredients:

225 g/8 oz/2 cups beef suet, shredded

225 g/8 oz/2 cups self-raising flour

225 g/8 oz/4 cups fresh white breadcrumbs

225 g/8 oz/1¼ cups stoned prunes, chopped finely

225 g/8 oz/1¼ cups currants

225 g/8 oz/1¼ cups raisins

225 g/8 oz/1¼ cups sultanas

225 g/8 oz/1 generous cup soft, dark brown sugar

110 g/4 oz/½ cup glacé (candied) cherries, washed and chopped

110 g/4 oz/½ cup mixed (candied) peel, chopped

1 cooking apple, peeled and grated

1 carrot, peeled and grated

1 lemon, grated zest and juice

1 orange, grated zest and juice

6 medium-sized eggs, beaten

1 teasp mixed spice/allspice

½ teasp nutmeg, grated

½ teasp cinnamon, ground

1 teasp salt

300 ml/10 fl oz/1¼ cups stout

Method:

Sift the flour. Mix flour, suet, breadcrumbs, dried fruits and sugar together. Stir in the salt, spices, peel, cherries, carrot and apple. Mix in eggs, stout, orange, lemon rind and juice.

Fill mixture into bowls, leaving 5cm (2 inches) headspace for rising. Cover with two layers of greaseproof paper, leaving a pleat in the centre. Tie tightly, arranging a handle on the top for lifting from the pot. Top with foil. Place in a steamer or pot with the water coming half-way up the bowl. Steam for 6–7 hours, topping up with boiling water as needed.

For the individual, small puddings, place in a roasting tin (with water coming half-way up the containers) and steam in an oven set at 150°C/300°F/Gas 2 for 1½ hours.

To reheat. Cover with fresh paper and string. Steam a large pudding for 2–3 hours, individual ones for 1 hour.

Serve with plain, unsweetened whipped cream, or clotted cream, or an egg custard sauce (see recipe, p.63).

Cook's Tip:

Unless you have a big family or a large number of guests for Christmas, there will be leftover pudding to deal with. In Dublin, wedges of pudding are fried gently in butter until hot through.

A more interesting approach is to take about 225 g/8 oz cold pudding, crumbed as fine as possible, and mix into a litre of slightly softened ice cream. Refreeze at once.

Christmas Pudding

BAILEYS IRISH CREAM WATER ICE

Baileys Irish Cream liqueur was the first of its kind. Now there are half a dozen others. Baileys – on or off the rocks – is popular the world over and is also used in many desserts, including cheescake and trifle. Making a water ice with cream may sound like a contradiction, but the result, however contradictory, is delicious!

SERVES 8

Ingredients:

700 g/1½ lb/3½ cups caster sugar

2⅓ ltrs/4 pts/9¼ cups water

600 ml/20 fl oz/2½ cups Baileys (or other) Irish Cream liqueur

borage flowers (optional)

Method:

Make a syrup of the sugar and water by boiling together until it leaves a sticky film on the back of a metal spoon. Allow it to cool. Mix in the cream liqueur. Pour into your ice-cream maker and process until frozen. Serve slightly softened in glasses decorated with blue borage flowers. Do not keep for even a single day – the liqueur's flavour and aroma will be lost!

FRESH CHEESE WITH SOFT SUMMER FRUITS

Once this dish would have been made at home from cooked buttermilk and a little fresh cream. Today fresh curd cheese is soft, smooth, creamy, delicate in taste and rather lighter in texture than commercial cream cheeses. In Ireland it may be made from cows' or goats' milk.

SERVES 4

Ingredients:

225 g/8 oz/1 cup fresh curd cheese

480 g/1 lb/3 cups strawberries or raspberries, or loganberries, or soft fruit of your choice, washed, hulled, and (if necessary) sliced

2–3 tablesp fresh cream

2 tablesp caster sugar

Method:

Beat the cheese, cream and sugar together until well mixed. Set some fruit aside for decoration. If you're using strawberries, slice them thinly. In a serving dish (or individual serving dishes, or glasses) layer the fruit with the cheese mixture. Top with the whole fruits. Chill before serving.

Strawberries & Raspberries

CARRAGEEN BLANCMANGE

The Irish always made use of a few of the many seaweeds available around our shores. Dillisk needs long cooking and was always chopped and served mixed through mashed potatoes. Sloke, which needs up to five hours cooking, was served as a vegetable with seafoods, with boiled bacon, and with lamb which had been finished on sea-grass pastures.

Carrageen remains popular today and can be bought ready-prepared. It is a valuable jellying agent widely used by commercial food processors and is also used in the manufacture of ice cream, beer and medicines. In home cooking, it's a light, fat-free, thickening agent for soups (particularly seafood ones). It is still a traditional cure for chesty coughs and colds, especially in children. Carageen jelly or blancmange was a widely used base for Victorian desserts and is making a sustained comeback in fine dining establishments.

SERVES 4

Ingredients:

15 g/½ oz dried carrageen moss

700 ml/23 floz/3³/₈ cups full-fat, fresh milk

1 tablesp sugar (or to taste)

1 vanilla pod

Method:

Work the dried carrageen very gently under cold, running water until it becomes just soft and pliable. Put it in a pan with the milk, vanilla pod and sugar, then simmer over a medium heat until virtually all the carrageen has dissolved. Strain into a bowl to remove any small pieces of tougher seaweed that remain. Pour the strained liquid into small ramekins or into a large decorative jelly mould and allow to set in a cool place.

Serve with seasonal fruit: strawberries, raspberries, or a mixed soft fruit compote of redcurrants, blackcurrants, white currants, blackberries, loganberries (or other similar soft fruits). A crisp biscuit provides a pleasant contrast in texture.

PANCAKES WITH FRESH RASPBERRIES AND CREAM

Pancakes are traditionally eaten in Ireland on Shrove Tuesday (the day before Lent begins). The Christian Church prescribed a rigorous period of fast and abstinence during the six weeks of Lent. This meant no animal products of any kind. Pancakes were made to use up all the eggs, butter and milk before the fast. Wild raspberries were once gathered by hunter-gatherers and have been cultivated in Ireland for millennia. Being especially suited to the Irish climate they grow well, even in bad summers. Of all the berries they are the most easily damaged and their fragrance fades fast – in other words, they are best straight from the cane. In my garden I have to beat off the wild deer from this favourite treat of theirs.

SERVES 10–12

Ingredients:

110 g/4 oz/1 cup plain white flour

125 ml/4 fl oz/½ cup milk

125 ml/4 fl oz/½ cup water

1 tablesp melted butter

2 medium-sized eggs, beaten

Method:

Sift the flour, then, using an electric whisk, beat in the eggs until you have a thick paste. Gradually whisk in the milk and water. You should end up with a mixture like thin cream. Allow to stand for a while.

Pick over the raspberries. Raspberries become soggy if washed, so it's best to do so only if absolutely necessary and then dry them well on absorbent kitchen paper. If you wish, sprinkle with caster sugar, but well-ripened raspberries hardly need it. Whip the cream lightly (adding a little sugar if you wish).

Heat a light pancake pan until quite hot. Dip folded kitchen paper in the butter and use it to lightly grease the pan. Pour about 2 tablespoons of the mixture into the pan, tilting it rapidly from side to side so that the batter spreads evenly. Cook over medium heat until the surface has bubbles and the underside is brown. Turn with a palette knife and cook the other side. Keep warm on a plate set over hot water. To serve, place on warm plates, spoon a few raspberries and a little cream on each. Fold over and top with a swirl of cream and a few more raspberries. Eat as soon as possible.

Variations:

Fresh strawberries are an obvious choice: wash, hull, dry, then slice into a little fresh orange juice (or white wine) to give a juicy filling.

Pretty well any fruit in season, skinned, stoned, and prepared as the fruit demands. Some fruits, like gooseberries, blackcurrants, or blackberries may need to be stewed gently and sweetened.

Pancakes are also good simply dressed with butter and lemon juice and served with sugar, honey or maple syrup.

SYLLABUB WITH BLUEBERRY PURÉE

Blueberries are cultivated in Ireland, often on cut-away bogs. They have a bittersweet taste and are in season in late summer. Wild blueberries, known as fraughans, are also plentiful and were traditionally picked on the first Sunday in August, called Blueberry (or Blaeberry) Sunday. Traditional syllabub is flavoured with wine or sherry. This is a fruity spin on an ancient dish.

SERVES 6

Ingredients:

450 g/1 lb blueberries

2 tablesp water

juice of one lemon

caster sugar to taste

300 ml/10 fl oz/1¼ cup cream

3 egg whites

crystallised violet flowers (optional) as a decoration

Method:

Reserve a few whole, raw fruits for decoration. Cook the rest gently in water and lemon juice until soft. Add sugar to taste and stir until it has dissolved. Purée through a mouli or in a food processor. Whip cream until thick but not stiff. In another bowl whip egg whites until fairly stiff. Very gently mix both together. Take six white wine glasses (flutes) and divide the fruit purée equally between them. Swirl equal quantities of the cream and egg white mixture on top. Decorate with a blueberry or a crystallised flower and chill for at least 2 hours before serving.

Serve with thin ginger biscuits.

FRUIT COMPOTE

Simple to make and very versatile, fruit compote can be eaten as a fruit dish at breakfast (with or without yoghurt), as a dessert with cream, or as a topping for porridge.

SERVES 4

Ingredients:

450 g/1 lb soft fruits in season (strawberries, raspberries, loganberries, black, red, or white currants, gooseberries, cherries, fraughans, or blackberries)

90 g/3 oz/(generous) ½ cup caster sugar (exact amount depends on preference and the relative tartness of the fruit)

Method:

Place the fruit in a heavy-based pot; stir in the sugar and warm gently over a low heat. As the juice begins to run, raise the heat so that it begins to simmer. Cook for about 2 minutes until the sugar is fully dissolved. Remove from the heat and cool.

Variation:

A soft fruit salad is similar except that a hot sugar syrup is poured directly over the fruit. Make this syrup by putting the pared rind and juice of an orange into 60 ml/2 fl oz/¼ cup of water with 60 g/2 oz/(scant) ¼ cup sugar; boil for 3 minutes, or until it has the consistency of a light syrup.

Strawberries & Raspberries

DRIED FRUIT COMPOTE

In Country House Hotels and Guest Houses you will often find this health-giving and rich compote on breakfast buffets. It's an easily-made and practical dish that provides vitamins when fresh fruit is scarce.

SERVES 6

Ingredients:

110 g/4 oz/¾ cup sultanas

110 g/4 oz/1 cup prunes, stoned and halved

350 g/12 oz/2¼ cups (ready to eat) dried apricots, halved

110 g/4 oz/1 cup almonds, flaked

½ teasp mixed spice/allspice

grated rind and juice of 1 orange

250 ml/8 fl oz/1 cup water

4 tablesp dry sherry (optional)

Method:

Place all the fruit in a bowl. Heat the water with the mixed spice, orange juice and rind to simmering point. Pour over the fruit and place in the fridge overnight. Top with flaked almonds and eat plain, or with yoghurt, with cream, or as a topping for porridge.

Selection of Dried Fruit

fRUIT fOOL

Gooseberries, rhubarb, raspberries and strawberries are favoured fruits for this simple concoction that has been popular for centuries. Today the health-conscious make a puréed fruit dessert using yoghurt which, while it bears little resemblance to a real fool in taste, is similar in texture.

SERVES 4

Ingredients:

450 g/1 lb fruit of your choice

60 ml/2 fl oz/¼ cup (or less) of water

caster sugar to taste

450 ml/15 floz/(scant) 2 cups of double cream

Method:

Stew the fruit in the water, adding just a little sugar at the start and adjusting the amount when the fruit is cooked. Cook until barely tender. Mash, or whiz in a food processor (use a mouli for raspberries, whose seeds do not respond well to being electrically processed). Check for sweetness. Allow the fruit to become completely cold. Whip the cream until it stands in peaks then fold into the fruit. Chill well before serving. Garnish the top with a few whole fruits.

BRACK AND BUTTER PUDDING

This variation on the well-loved bread and butter pudding uses the traditional Irish Hallowe'en tea cake – barm brack – which gives a richer, spicier flavour to the pudding.

SERVES 4

Ingredients:

225 g/8 oz brack (see recipe p.78)

750 ml/1¼ pints/3 US cups milk

60 g/2 oz/½ stick butter

6 eggs

3 egg yolks

60 g/2 oz/(scant) ¼ cup sugar

2 teasp vanilla essence

Method:

Cut the brack into slices about 1cm/½ inch thick; cut these in half and butter. Take a large shallow dish (about 1.75 litres/3 pint capacity), grease it with butter, then arrange the slices of brack in it, buttered side up, overlapping just a little. Mix together the eggs, egg yolks, sugar, vanilla essence, and milk, and strain this over the slices of brack. Allow to stand in a cool place for half an hour. Place the dish in a water bath (a roasting tin about half-filled with hot water) and bake at 170°C/325°F/Gas 3 for about an hour (or until the custard is set). Serve hot.

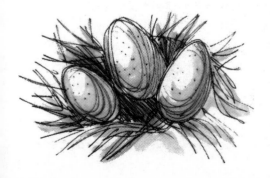

IRISH FARMHOUSE CHEESES

Bánbhianna (*white foods*) were summer foods that, according to an English traveller passing through Ireland in 1690, were eaten 'in twenty several different sorts of ways'. First there was butter and its by-product buttermilk; then various thickened milks. The English gave a collective name to these drinks – clabber. Clabbering was the process of souring and thickening the milk, sometimes with rennet, sometimes with sorrel, or butterwort juice. These drinks, together with cheeses, formed a substantial part of the Irish diet until the close of the seventeenth century.

Butter (*for export*) and buttermilk lingered on but the cheeses became no more than literary and historical references. Grutha was a collective name for curd cheeses – Fáiscre grotha was a pressed curd; Tanach was a hard cheese described in the vision as 'sleek pillars of ripe cheese' holding up the roof of a building; and Maethal was a smooth, sweet, soft cheese. The latter was large, too, another writer describing a person of large girth says, 'his buttocks were like half a maethal'. Grús was a kneaded soft cheese made from soured buttermilk; Milsén was a semi-liquid curd cheese; and, the one that survived the longest, Mulchán, was a hard cheese made from skimmed milk, which was still being made and exported from Waterford in 1824. Gradually, historical and economic factors caused a slow but inexorable decline in cheese eating and cheesemaking in Ireland. A century later, to use up milk surpluses, agricultural co-operatives began to manufacture 'creamery cheeses' with great success, exporting mainly a cheddar-type cheese all over the world.

Thirty years ago a new generation of farmhouse cheesemakers began a magnificent revival of this ancient tradition. Although the new Irish cheesemakers took their technology from mainland Europe, what astounds European visitors today is that all our farmhouse cheeses are unique to their maker. Visitors find it eccentric that each cheese is produced on one farm by one family and is as they say in Ireland 'entirely itself'. What is common to all of them is Irish milk. Our climate allows cows, goats, *and sheep to be out on green, well-watered grass for nine months of the year and to feed on natural grass fodder in winter. There are over three score farmhouse cheesemakers today. Curiously, not a single one has chosen to use an old name for their cheese. But they are, nevertheless, 'historic' in the modern sense of the word.*

A cheeseboard is the ideal way to appreciate the range and individuality of Irish farmhouse cheeses. Choose at least three cheeses offering a variety of tastes, textures, strengths and colour. Offer them in order of strength; the mildest first, working towards the strongest. The following combinations I find especially pleasing:

1. *Mine Gabhar* from Croghan Goat Farm – a natural rind cheese, silky, slightly sweet, with oaky, herbal flavours. *Coolea* is a Gouda-style cheese; semi-firm at 6 months, with a complex sweet-sour taste with herb and grassy hints. As it ages, the texture becomes firm and the taste heavier and more robust. *Ardrahan* is a rustic golden-brown washed rind, semi-firm cheese; its earthy, smoky flavour grows more robust as it ages. *Desmond* and *Gabriel* from the West Cork Cheese Company are made in Swiss alpage-style. *Desmond* is the more intense, with spicy flavours balanced by floral elements. *Gabriel*, though more delicate, is still intense, sweeter, more subtle. At 8 months they have a moist, dense texture. At 2 years this becomes granular and flinty.

2. *Knockalara* is a fresh, moist sheep's cheese; a delicate taste with hints of citrus and herbs. *Knockanore* is hard-pressed, the flavour has depth and presence and takes on a long tang when well-aged. *Cashel Blue* has its own buttery-sweet tang. Eaten at about 4 months, it becomes a rich yellow and turns buttery. *Milleens* has a mottled peach, sometimes fiery orange, washed rind. It develops from semi-firm to flowing cream with a complex flavour of herbs with a spicy tang.

3. *Boilie* Goats Cheese from Ryefield Farm is soft, fresh and aromatic. *Dilliskus* is a hard cheese, packed with taste that is not overwhelmed by the flavour of dillisk – a seaweed traditional to Irish food culture. *Crozier Blue*, a sheep's milk cheese from the makers of Cashel Blue, has a pronounced, smooth flavour and a thick, buttery texture. *Cooleeney* is a velvety, melting Camembert-type. When ripe it has a smooth, robust flavour with a tangy finish. *Durrus* is a washed rind cheese. It has an earthy flavour and a velvety, moist texture.

BARM BRACK

Brack, our traditional fruit bread, has been a festive dish since ancient times. It was eaten at Lughnasa, the first day of autumn and the start of the harvest, at Samhain, the first day of winter, and on February 1ˢᵗ, St Brigid's Day, the first day of spring. All Souls' Night (Hallowe'en) may now have supplanted the pre-Christian festival of Samhain, but it's still the night on which brack is always eaten in Ireland. A ring is placed in the brack to herald marriage the following spring for whoever finds it. In Cork (always wanting to go one better) they also put in a pea for spinsterhood, a bean for riches, a rag for poverty, and a piece of matchstick, which predicts that your husband will beat you! There are two versions of the origin of the name barm brack: that it comes from the Irish bairgain breac – bread that is speckled; the other that it derives from the use of barm, or yeast drawn off fermenting malt. Brack made at home, as often as not, is raised not with yeast but with baking powder and is called a tea brack because the dried fruit is soaked in tea. A barm brack, on the other hand, is raised with yeast (but not barm) and is bought from a bakery. Both types are eaten sliced and buttered.

Ingredients:

255 g/9 oz/1 ¼ cups raisins

255 g/9 oz/1 ½ cups sultanas

60 g/2 oz/(scant) ¼ cup mixed peel (optional)

225 g/8 oz/(generous) 1 cup dark cane sugar

500 ml/16 fl oz/2 cups Indian tea, hot, strong and black

350 g/12 oz/3 cups of plain white flour

2 teasp baking powder

2 medium-sized eggs, beaten

a little honey for the glaze

a 20 cm/8 inch cake tin at least 7.5 cm/3 inches deep, greased and lined with greaseproof (unwaxed) or non-stick paper

Method:

Place the fruit, sugar and peel in a bowl and pour the hot tea (without milk) over them; stir well until the sugar is dissolved, then stand overnight. Sift flour, baking powder and spice. Mix, alternately, some egg and some fruit into the flour, stirring thoroughly. When all the egg and fruit has been mixed in, add the ring and other charms if you are using them, making sure that they are evenly distributed through the mix. For safety, wrap them in greasproof paper. Turn out the mixture into the prepared cake tin and bake at 160°C/325°F/Gas 3 for about 1½ hours. About 10 minutes before it is ready, brush the top of the brack with warmed honey. Return to the oven until fully cooked. Cool in the tin for 15 minutes before turning out on to a rack (glazed side up) to cool. It keeps well in a tin for 4–5 days.

Cook's Tip:

Leftover brack may be used for the rich Brack and Butter Pudding on p. 76. It is also very good toasted and buttered.

Barm brack

potato apple farls

A 'farl' is a triangular shape whose name (fardel) originally meant a fourth part of anything. This rough triangle cut from a circle is the traditional shape for potato cakes and griddle bread as well as for these rather unusual apple pastries. In some parts of the country they were served at Hallowe'en with the ring or 'favour' placed in just one cake. Originally they would have been cooked on a griddle over an open turf fire. They can be cooked on a heavy frying pan and can also be baked in a hot oven.

MAKES 4

Ingredients:

480 g/1 lb/4 cups white flour

480 g/1 lb/3 generous cups floury potatoes, mashed while hot

15 g/½ oz/1 tablesp butter, melted

½ teasp baking powder

4 large cooking apples (Bramley for preference) peeled, cored, and thinly sliced

honey or brown sugar, and butter, to taste

Method:

Mix the sifted flour and baking powder in a bowl; add the melted butter and the hot, mashed potatoes. Mix well, then knead lightly until you have a soft dough. Divide into two equal pieces.

Roll out the dough on a floured board until you have a circle 1cm/½-inch thick. Divide into four farls (triangles). Repeat with the other piece of dough. On each of four farls place an equal amount of the apple, then place another farl on top. Pinch the edges together to seal them well.

Cook over a medium heat on a griddle (or in a heavy frying pan) until brown on the bottom. Turn carefully and brown the other side. Now comes the tricky bit! Slit the pastries horizontally and lift off the tops. Add thin slices of butter and (depending how sweet you like your dessert) as much honey and/or sugar as you fancy. Carefully replace the tops and continue cooking for a few minutes until the butter and sugar have melted into a sauce. Serve hot.

kerry apple cake

Kerry men (and women and children) are well known inside and outside Ireland for having jokes told against them. Actually, I've always regarded this as the best Kerry joke of all because, in reality, Kerry people are famous for being 'cute' – clever, on the ball, always keeping the best things secret. In a Kerry apple cake the apples are 'invisible', their presence revealed only when you taste it.

SERVES 4–8

Ingredients:

3 large cooking apples, peeled, cored and diced

225 g/8 oz/2 cups white flour

110 g/3 oz/¾ stick butter

110 g/3 oz/(scant) ½ cup caster sugar

1 teasp baking powder

¼ teasp salt

1 extra-large egg, beaten

¼ teasp nutmeg, grated (or ground cinnamon or ground cloves)

3 tablesp Demerara sugar

Method:

Grease a 20cm (8-inch) cake tin with butter then line it with greaseproof paper.

Sift the flour into a bowl and rub in the butter until you have a mixture like fine breadcrumbs. Mix the salt, sugar, and baking powder together in a small bowl then stir into the flour mixture. Add the chopped apples and the egg and mix to a soft dough. Turn the dough into the cake tin. Mix the sugar and spice and sprinkle over the top of the cake. Bake at once at 180°C/350°F/Gas 4 for about 45 minutes, or until a skewer inserted into the middle of the cake comes out clean. Traditionally this cake is eaten hot from the oven. It can be served warm (even cold) as long as it is freshly made – just warm it gently if it is to be eaten the following day.

TOPLESS MINCE PIES

Mince pies were originally made in an oval shape to represent the manger in which the child Jesus was laid. They were filled with minced beef and suet and flavoured with three spices: cloves, mace, and pepper, as a reminder of the gifts brought by the three wise men. Tradition had it that twelve pies should be eaten between Christmas Day and the Twelfth Day of Christmas to ensure good luck in the year ahead. Mincemeat nowadays contains no meat at all and is a sweet preserve made with dried fruits, suet, spices, and usually contains alcohol. This is a modern recipe, lighter and less indigestible than pies made with flaky pastry.

MAKES 12

Ingredients:

350 g/12 oz/3 cups plain white flour

225 g/8 oz/2 sticks unsalted butter

90 g/3 oz/(scant) 1 cup ground almonds

90 g/3 oz/(scant) ½ cup caster sugar

2 egg yolks

2 tablesp very cold water

450 g/1 lb/2 cups high quality mincemeat

90 g/3 oz/¾ cup icing (confectioner's) sugar

a few drops of almond essence

a few drops of water

Method:

Make the pastry by sifting the flour and rubbing in the butter until it resembles breadcrumbs. Stir in the almonds, caster sugar, egg yolks and just sufficient water to make a paste. Wrap in cling film and chill for 1 hour. Roll out thinly (3mm/⅛ inch thick) and cut into circles with a 7.5cm (3 inch) fluted cutter. Place in greased patty tins and spoon one teaspoon of mincemeat into each base. Take care not to overfill lest the filling bubble over the edges as it cooks. Bake at 200°C/400°F/Gas 6 for about 15 minutes. Cool in the tin for 5 minutes, then transfer to a wire rack to cool. Make the icing by sifting icing (confectioner's) sugar, adding a drop or two of almond essence and just sufficient water to get a pouring consistency. Drizzle over the top of the pies with a zig-zag, to-and-fro motion. Once the icing has set they are ready to eat.

PORTER CAKE

Porter was a type of stout, weaker in alcohol content but with the same dark colour and rich flavour as present day stouts. Alas, porter is no longer available (nor has it been for many a long year) so, although we now make this cake with stout, it's still called porter cake! Like many Irish dishes there is no definitive recipe — every province, county, parish, townland, house (and even the women within that house) puts its own spin on the recipe. This particular recipe is that of Paula Daly, a famous Irish cook, who, through the medium of radio, taught many an Irish cook not to fear baking!

Ingredients:

175 g/6 oz/1 generous cup wholemeal flour

175 g/6 oz/1½ cups plain white flour,

1 teasp (rounded) mixed spice/allspice

1 teasp (level) baking powder

225 g/8 oz/(generous) 1 cup soft dark brown sugar

225 g/8 oz /2 sticks butter

3 large eggs, beaten

250 ml/8 fl oz/1 cup stout (Guinness, Beamish, or Murphy's)

175 g/6 oz/(generous) 1 cup raisins

175 g/6 oz/1 cup sultanas

90 g/3 oz/¾ cup walnuts, chopped

grated rind of an orange

Method:

Put the wholemeal flour in a bowl and sift the white flour, mixed spice and baking powder on top. Mix well. In another bowl, cream the butter and sugar until very light and fluffy. Add the eggs, a little at a time, beating well during and after each addition. Should the mixture curdle add a little flour. Gradually fold in the flour and stout, a little at a time. When everything is incorporated fold in the fruit, nuts, and orange rind. Turn into a tin (20cm/8 inches square, or 23cm/9 inches round) lined with greaseproof (unwaxed) paper. Smooth the top evenly with the back of a tablespoon, then bake on a low shelf in a preheated oven at 150°C/300°F/Gas 2 for 3¼–3½ hours.

Porter Cake

ḣOT CROSS BUNS

Traditionally eaten on Good Friday, the Friday before Easter Sunday. The cross on the top is the Christian symbol, a reminder that this was the day Jesus was crucified.

MAKES 12

Ingredients:

For the dough:

450 g/1 lb/4 cups strong white flour

1 teasp quick-action yeast

a good pinch of salt

½ teasp ground cinnamon,

1 teasp mixed spice/allspice

¾ teasp nutmeg, grated

90 g/3 oz/½ cup sultanas

90 g/3 oz/(scant) ½ cup currants

30 g/1 oz/1 tablesp mixed (candied) peel, chopped (optional)

1 medium-sized egg, beaten

250 ml/8 fl oz/1 cup full-fat milk

For the crosses:

2 tablesp butter

45 g/1½ oz/⅓ cup flour

a little cold water

Method:

Mix the flour, yeast, salt, spices and dried fruit together. Add the egg and enough milk to make a soft dough (you may need more or less liquid). Knead the dough until really smooth to the touch and elastic in texture; by hand this will take 10 minutes, using dough hooks and an electric mixer rather less time (and considerably less effort). Divide into 12 pieces and shape into round buns. Place on a well-greased baking tray leaving enough room for each bun to expand. Cover and prove at (warm) room temperature until they have risen and reached twice their original size.

Make the dough for the crosses by rubbing softened butter into flour and wetting with just enough water to make a soft dough. Roll out thinly and cut into narrow strips. Wet the underside of each strip and place two strips on each bun in the shape of a cross. Bake at 200°C/400°F/Gas 6 for 25–30 minutes. They should be well risen and browned, and when the bottom of a bun is tapped lightly, it should sound hollow. Serve freshly cooked, with butter.

BUTTERMILK SCONES

Scones are the great standby of an Irish country kitchen. They can be made in a few minutes and eaten warm from the oven. With imagination, a plain scone can be transformed into a variety of sweet and savoury breads.

MAKES 8–12

Ingredients:

450 g/1 lb/4 cups plain white flour

1 teasp (scant) bicarbonate of soda (bread soda)

1 teasp salt

80 g/3 oz/³/₄ stick butter, cubed

1 egg, beaten (optional)

about 175 ml/6 fl oz/¾ cup buttermilk

Method:

Sift the flour, salt, and bicarbonate of soda together. Rub in the butter until the texture resembles breadcrumbs. Quickly (and lightly) mix in the egg and milk, using just enough to make a soft dough that is puffy and easy to roll out. Knead lightly – no more than six times. Roll out to 2–2½cm/¾–1 inch thick (depending on how high and moist you prefer the finished scone). For even rising, cut out the scones with a fluted cutter dipped in flour, or with a very sharp knife. Transfer to a baking sheet with a palette knife. Bake immediately at 220°C/425°F/gas 7 for 15–20 minutes, or until well risen and brown.

Savoury Variations:

Use half plain white and half fine-ground wholemeal flour.

Add 175g/6 oz/1¼ cups grated hard cheese: extra mature Cheddar, Gabriel (from the West Cork Cheese Company), or Parmesan.

Brush with milk and sprinkle about 2 tablespoons of poppy seeds over the top.

Sweet Variations:

Fruit Scones: mix in 1 tablespoon of sugar and 3 or 4 tablespoons of sultanas.

Apple scones: mix in 1–2 finely chopped apples (peeled and cored) with a teaspoon of ground nutmeg (or cinnamon).

Apricot scones: add about 6 moist dried apricots, finely chopped.

GRIDDLE BREAD

At its best straight from the griddle and lavishly buttered. This bread, sliced and fried, is also an essential part of the Ulster Fry. In southern counties you're more likely to encounter it toasted. A contemporary spin is to use it as you would Greek pitta bread or Italian focaccia – split and filled with whatever filling takes your fancy.

MAKES 4

Ingredients:

450 g/1 lb/4 cups plain white flour

1 teasp salt

1 teasp bicarbonate of soda

500 ml/16 fl oz/2 cups buttermilk (you may need a little more or less)

Method:

Put the griddle (or a heavy-based frying pan) on the hob over a medium heat.

Sift the flour, soda and salt into a bowl. Pour in most of the buttermilk and mix as lightly as possible with your hands or a large spoon; use only enough milk to form a soft dough. Do not on any account use a food processor.

Turn the dough out onto a floured worktop, flour your hands and knead very lightly. Don't be tempted to knead soda bread as you would a yeast loaf – speed and lightness of touch is the essence of making Irish soda breads of all types. Knead with a circular movement while flipping in the outermost edge; stop immediately it all holds together. Roll out to about 1 cm/½ inch–3 cm/1½ inches thick (this is a matter of personal taste, regional variation, and how you plan to eat it). Cut into four farls or quarter-circles. You may separate them or leave them touching.

Before cooking, test the heat of the griddle or pan. It is at the correct temperature if a little flour sprinkled on it browns quickly. Thin griddle breads take about 6–7 minutes on each side at a medium heat.

The technique for thicker versions is different. As soon as you put the bread on the griddle turn the heat down to very low. Cook for 5 minutes. Then turn it up to medium-low and cook until lightly browned underneath. Cook the second side at the same heat until it too is browned. To check if it is sufficiently cooked, gently open one side. It should look dry right through.

Griddle Pan

BROWN SODA BREAD

Still called a brown 'cake' in many homes, and just brown bread in others, this is the national loaf. It is made with varying amounts of wholemeal and plain white flour and (depending on the mood of the cook) small amounts of extra ingredients like wheat germ, wheat bran, oatmeal, or various seeds. Sometimes a small amount of butter (or even an egg) is added and, occasionally, a little treacle/molasses. The exact amount of buttermilk required depends on the flour and the weather – I mean it!

Ingredients
For the basic bread:

450 g/1 lb/4 cups wholemeal wheat flour

175 g/6 oz/1½ cups plain white flour

1 teasp (generous) bicarbonate of soda

1 teasp salt

About 450 ml/15 fl oz /(scant) 2 cups buttermilk.

Method:

Pre-heat the oven to 200°C/400°F/Gas 6. The reaction of bicarbonate of soda and buttermilk is swift and the duration of their interaction short – speed is of the essence. Mix the flours, salt and soda in a mixing bowl. Add only enough buttermilk to make a soft dough. Flour your hands and the work surface and knead lightly (by hand, never with a machine) until the dough is smooth. It is important to understand that this is quite unlike making a yeast-risen dough. Shape into a circle about 4 cm/1½ inches deep. Take a sharp, well-floured knife and cut a deep cross in the top. Place on a baking sheet and bake for 40–45 minutes. To see if it is fully cooked test by tapping the bottom and listening for a hollow sound. Cool on a rack or, if you like a soft crust, wrapped in a linen or cotton tea-cloth. Eat the same day.

Variations:

White soda bread is made with all white plain flour. Curranty bread has about 110g/ 4 oz each of sultanas and currants added.

BEVERAGES

The Irish have been brewing and distilling since earliest times and had the climate been suitable we would have made wine. Since the Celts arrived, wine has been imported (as written records in Bordeaux attest). Early Christian monks sailed up the Loire to buy wine; Brian Boru was paid a tribute of wine by the Vikings — but, alas, wine was a reserved drink for Irish Kings and Irish monks! Interestingly, monks were allowed eight pints of ale a day, which sounds a lot, but it was a very weak brew. This also gave rise to the saying 'he's had one over the eight' of someone who has had too much to drink. The ordinary people drank home-brewed ale and cider, hot, cold, and flavoured with spices. At one feast in Ulster 1000 barrels were consumed and voices were raised in song so loudly that they disturbed the peace of Munster hundreds of miles to the south! Our three great beers were ale, porter, and stout — a dark, distinctive drink with a rich malt flavour. Mead, the primary schoolbook drink of heroes, was made from honey and always a rare delicacy.

The secret art of distilling was brought to Ireland from the Mediterranean some fifteen hundred years ago and developed into a drink called uisce beatha — the water of life. Irish missionary monks brought the process to Scotland where it eventually developed into the drink we know today as whisky (even the Scots don't dispute that the Irish invented whiskey). Once tax began to be levied on whisky (by Charles II) poitín was the Irish response. Despite the fact that it has always been illegal, it is still made today (both legally and illegally) and enjoyed all over the island. Sources are a most closely-guarded secret!

SLOE GIN

Sloes are the fruits of the blackthorn bush (from which comes the traditional shillelagh, or blackthorn stick). Deep purple-blue with a faint whitish bloom of natural yeasts, sloes ripen through late September and October. They are best picked after the first frosts, which soften the skins and aid the release of juice from the fruit. Nature, however, rarely provides perfect harvests. In medieval times monks used sloes to distil a drink similar to gin. Nowadays, because it is (sadly) illegal to distil spirits even for consumption at home, sloes are used to flavour commercial gins. An occasional, and illegal, treat is poitín made using sloes. Here are two legal recipes.

GIN FLAVOURED WITH SLOE AND ALMONDS

As well as adding a distinctive, bittersweet taste, the juice from the sloes turns ordinary gin a lovely shade of pink. Great on its own or in a cocktail.

MAKES 2X 75cl winebottles

Ingredients:

1 litre bottle of gin (preferably Cork Dry Gin but it could be Dutch Old Genever)

250 g/½ lb whole almonds, baked, or peeled kernels (or almond essence)

sufficient sloes to fill one 75cl wine bottle

Method:

Using a sharp fork prick each berry and drop it directly into one of two clean wine bottles. Half fill each bottle with sloes. Add the almond essence, or the whole baked almonds. Top up both bottles with gin. Cork them securely and store in a moderately warm place for 3 months to allow the flavour to develop. It will keep for at least a year.

SLOE GIN LIQUEUR

MAKES 1 litre bottle

Ingredients:

250 g/½ lb sloes

2 tablesp sugar

8 almonds, blanched and cracked

.75 litre bottle of gin

Method:

Prick the sloes and drop them at once into a clean dry gin bottle containing the sugar until you can fit no more. Fill the bottle with gin. Cork tightly and store in a warm place. It is usual to shake the bottle very gently once a week for about 3 months and then to let it stand (undisturbed) for a further 6 months. After that time, strain the liqueur through clean muslin into another (very clean) bottle and store in a dark place.

The liqueur will keep for a year.

bot whiskey punch

Also known as a 'hot toddy', this is a popular nightcap and a great drink to hold and sip on cold, damp winter evenings. Our family doctor (suitably old, gnarled and crusty) prescribes this (and bed rest) to my husband on the rare occasions he shows any signs of sickening for anything at all. It appears to be infallible!

Ingredients:

1 measure (37.5 ml/2½
tablesp) Irish whiskey
1 slice of lemon
3–4 whole cloves
boiling water
sugar (or honey) to taste

Method:

Warm the glass (preferably an Irish whiskey glass) by placing a teaspoon in it and pouring in just-boiled water. The spoon is essential because it absorbs the heat more quickly than the glass and prevents the glass cracking. Working quickly, empty the glass, add the whiskey, lemon, cloves, and sweetener. Press the lemon slice to release a little juice. Add boiling water to nearly fill the glass (or whatever amount of water is pleasing to your palate). Stir to dissolve the sweetening and sip while hot.